FLOWERS
COLORING BOOK

MY NAME IS:

_____

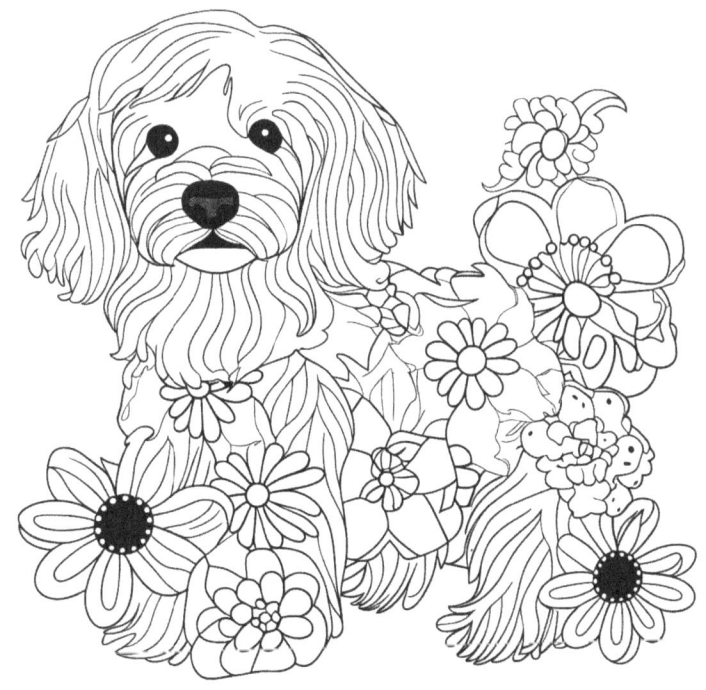

GARDEN

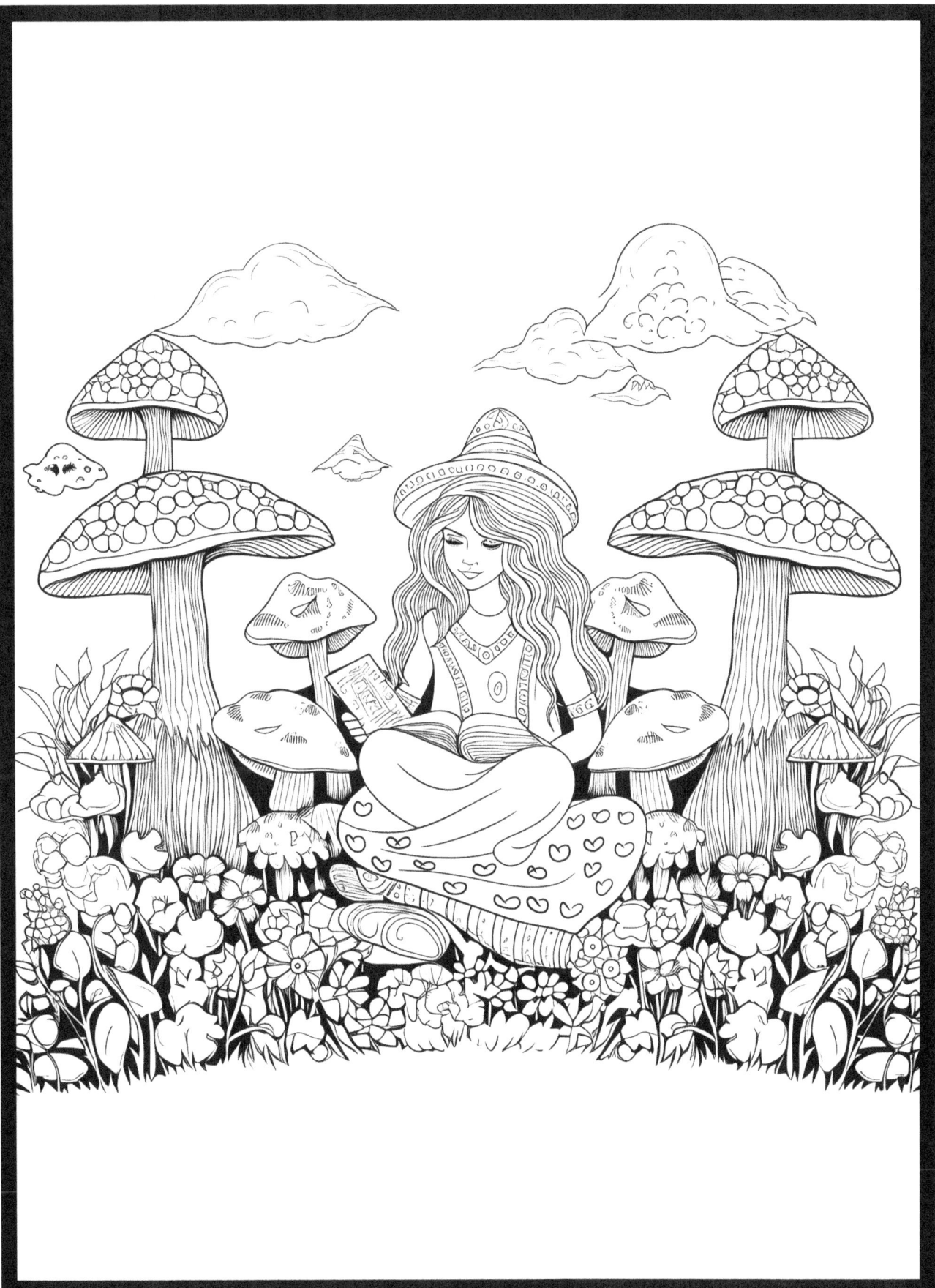

LION

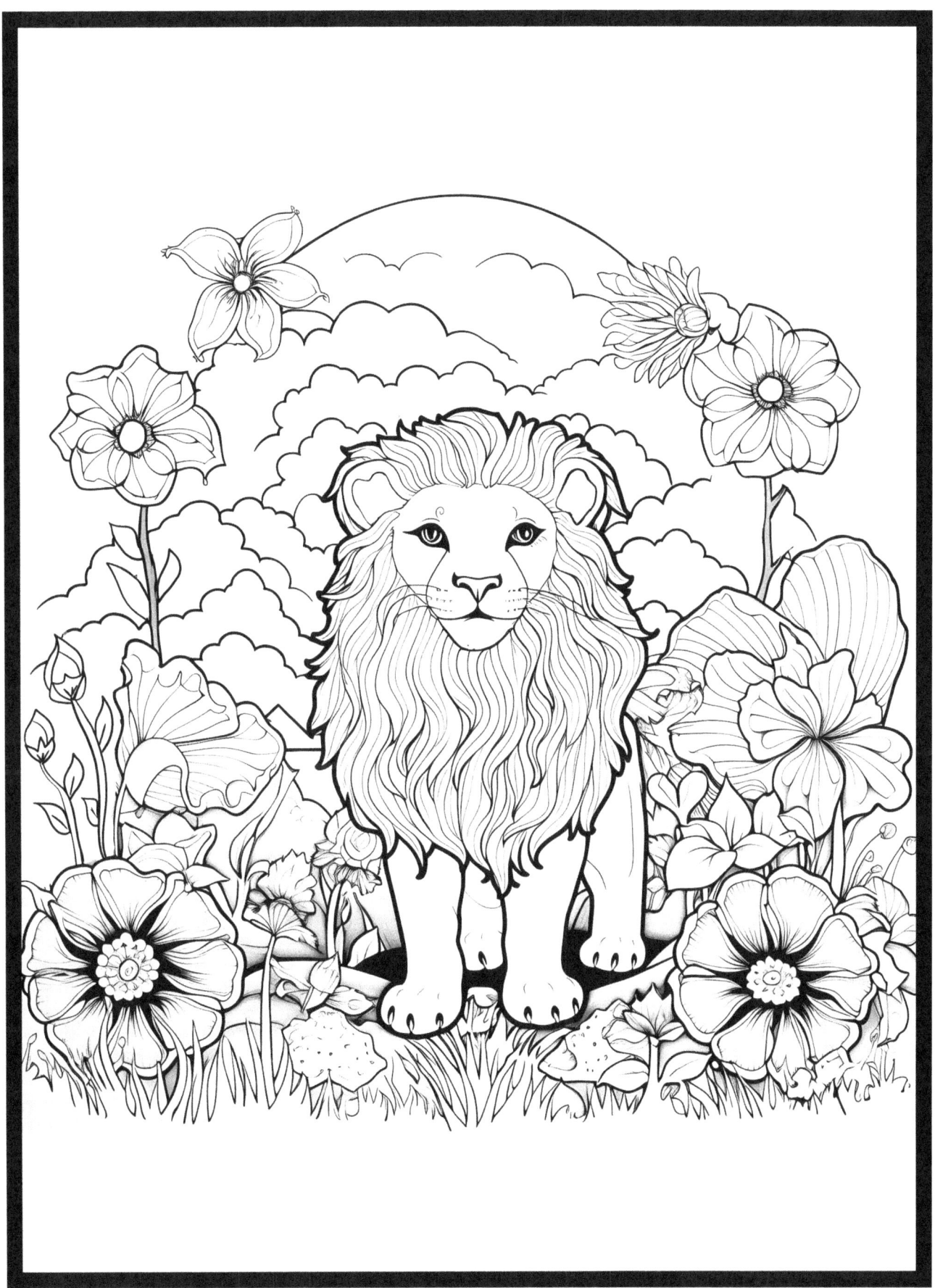

FLOWERS

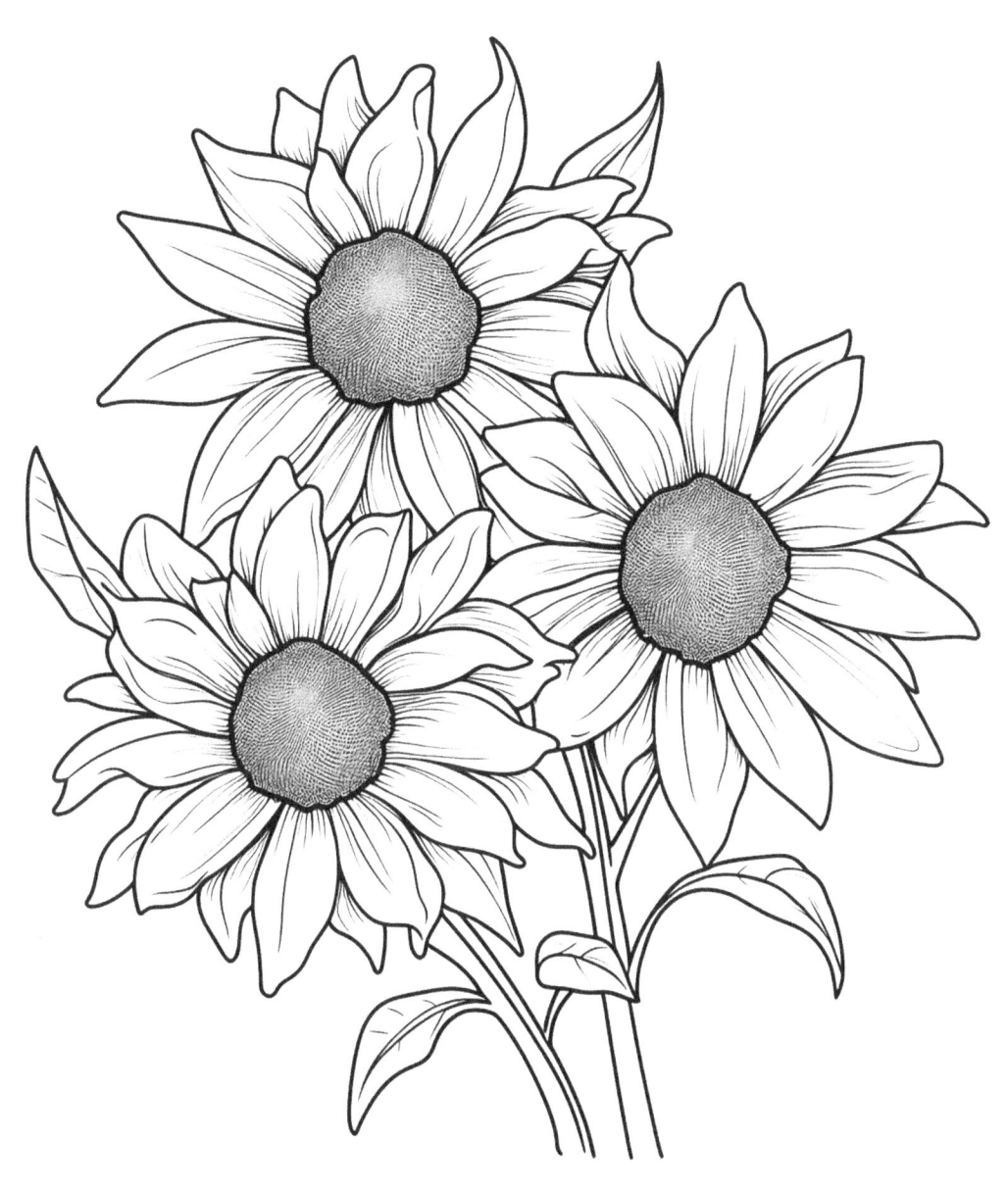

SNAKE

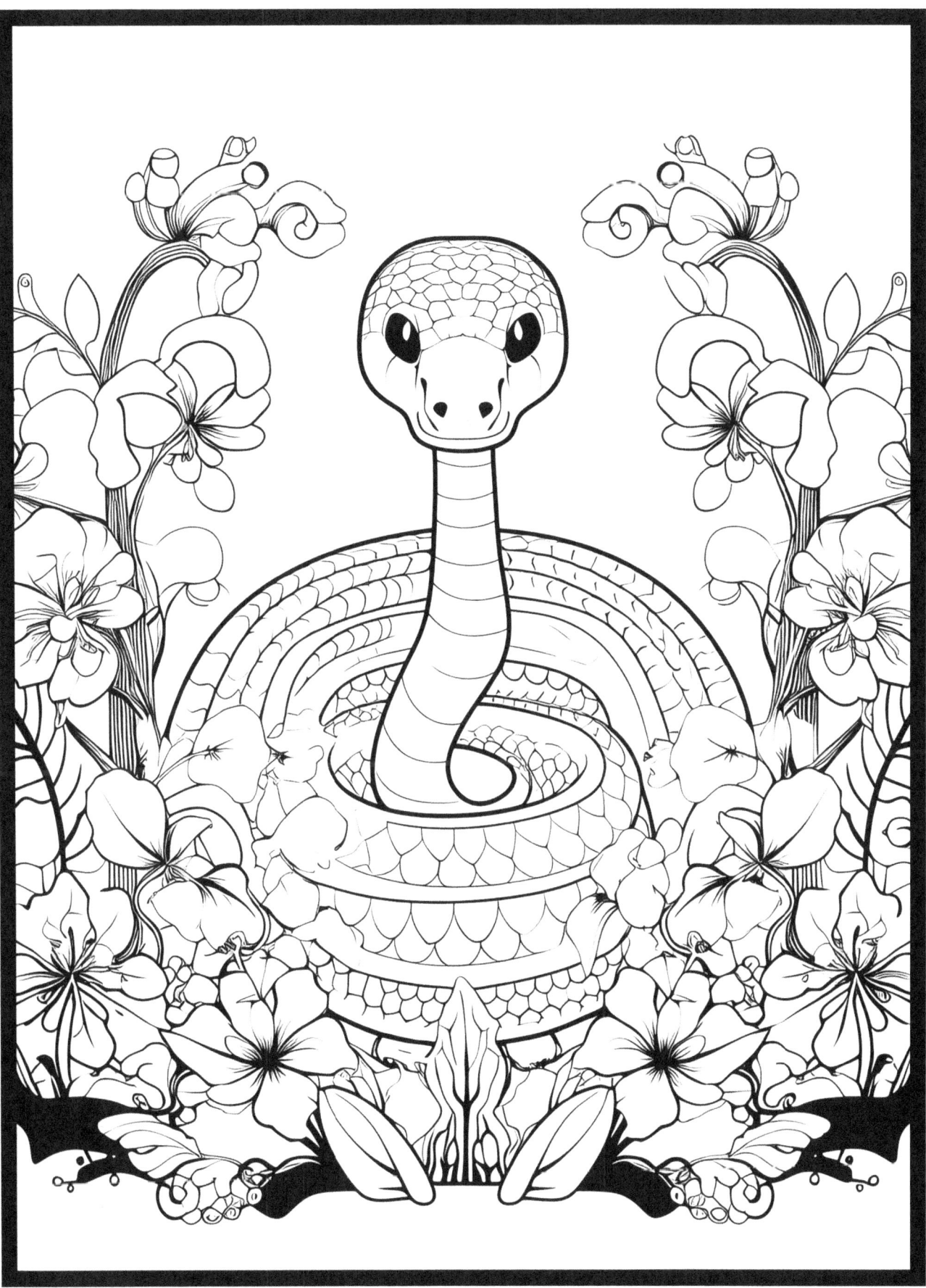

CAT

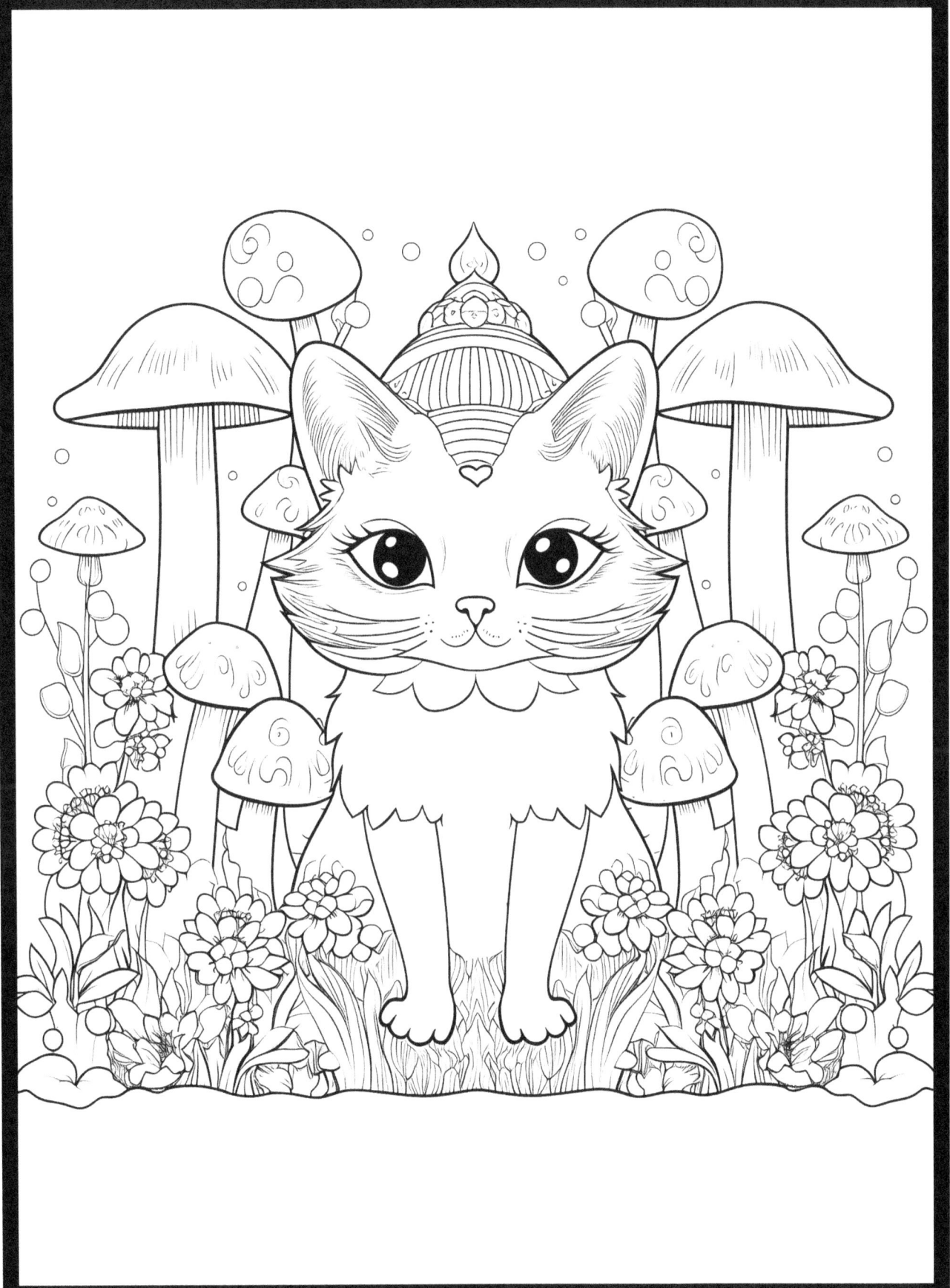

GIRL

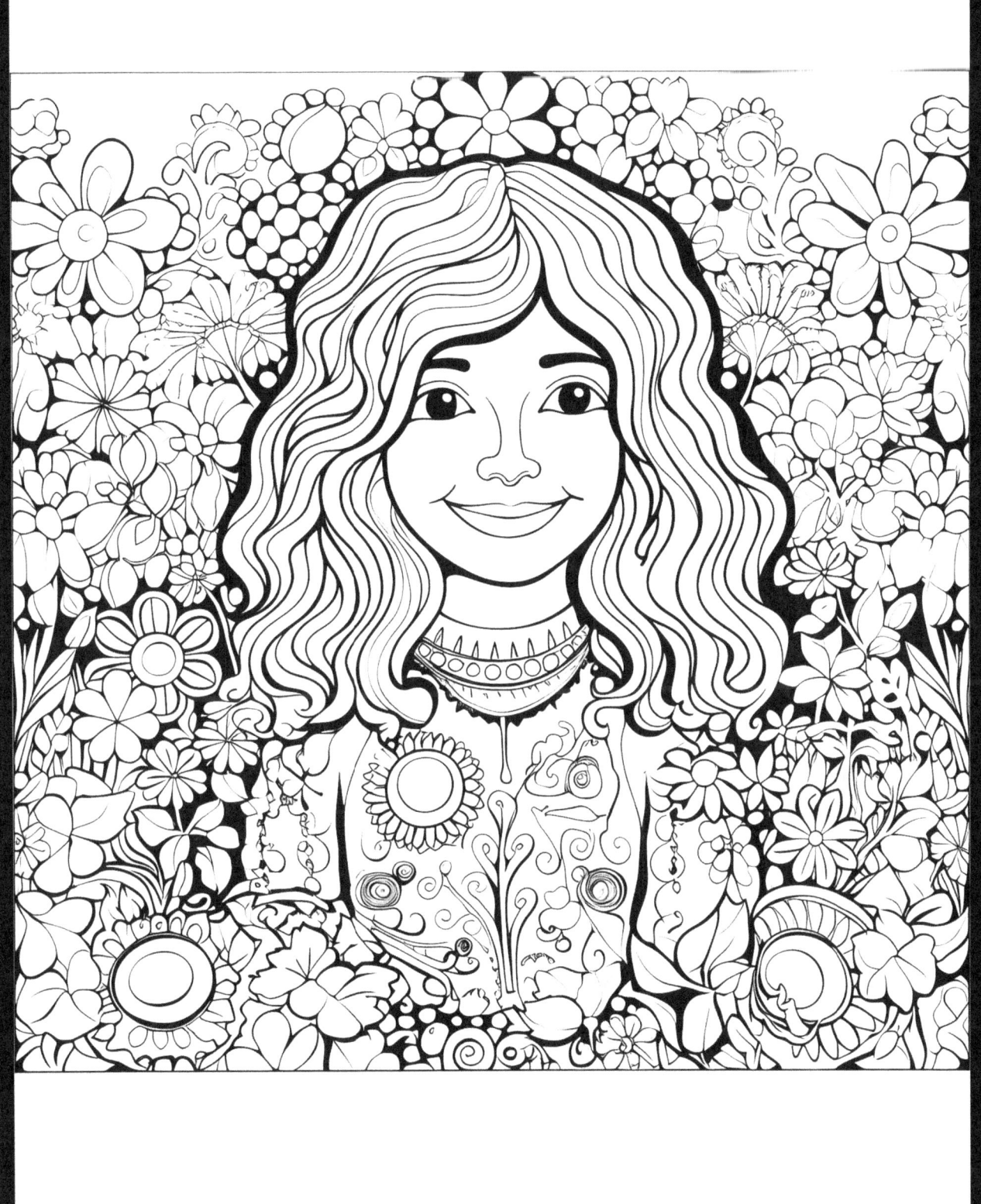

LITTLE HOUSE

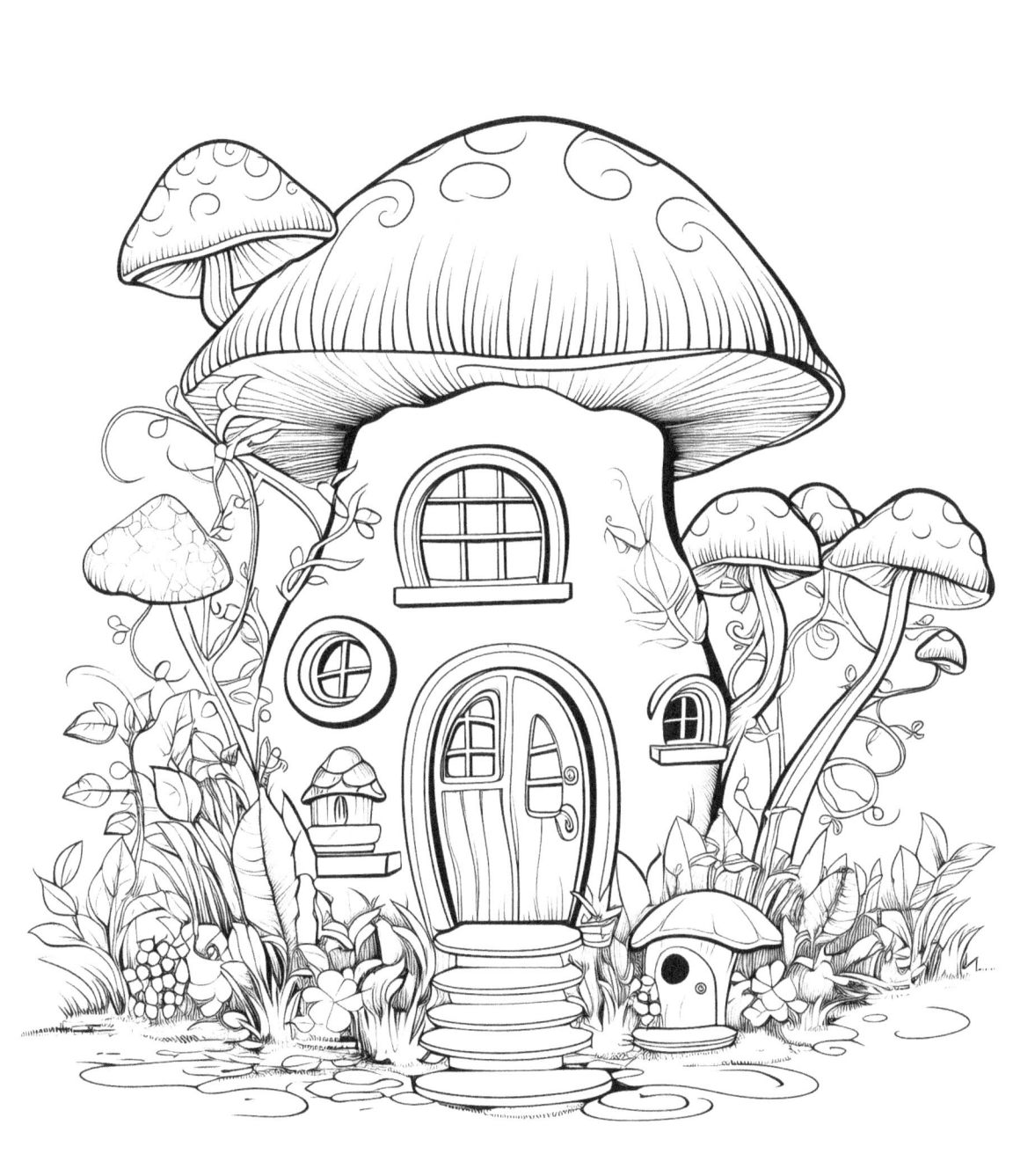

ROSES

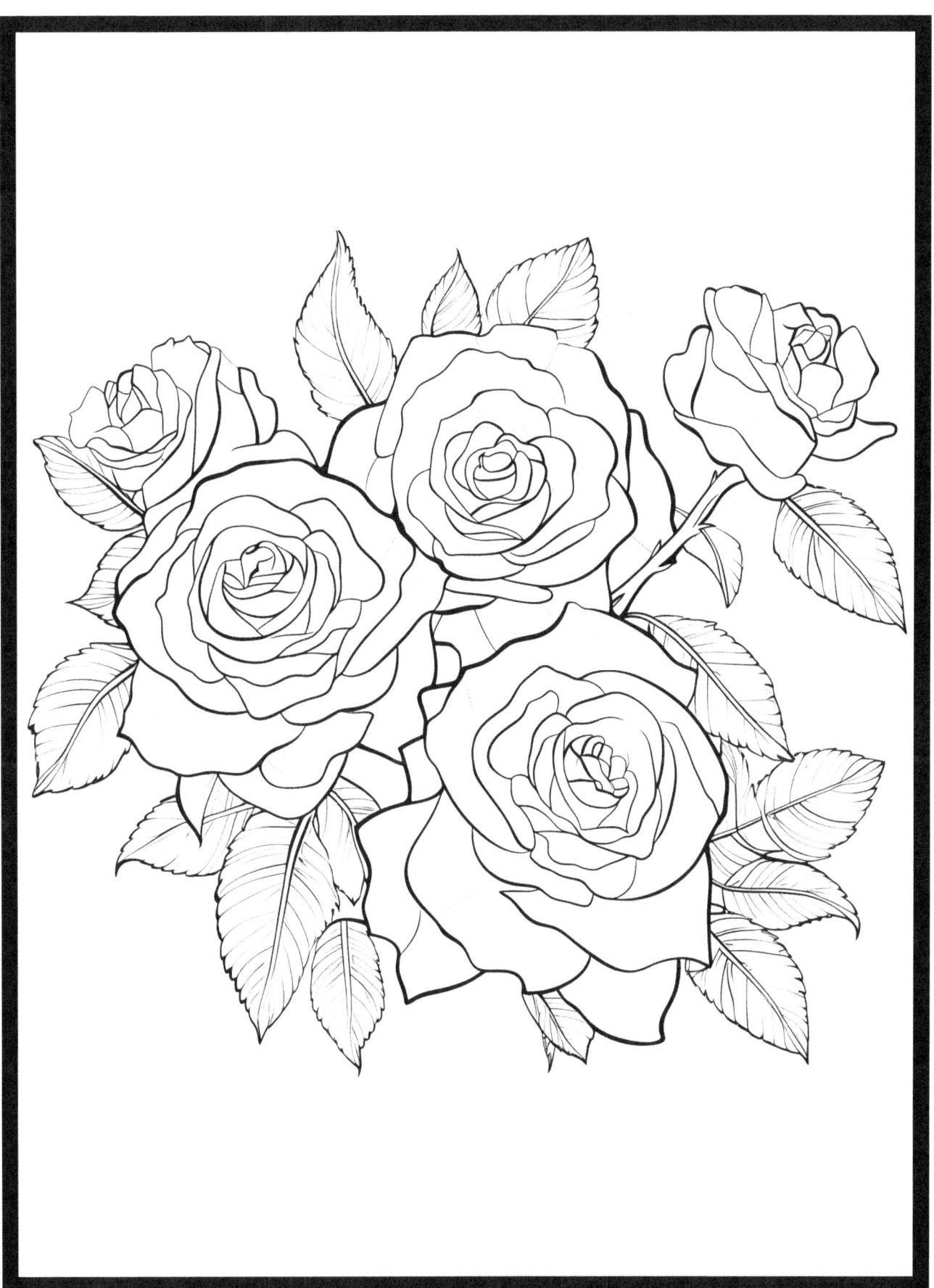

GUITAR

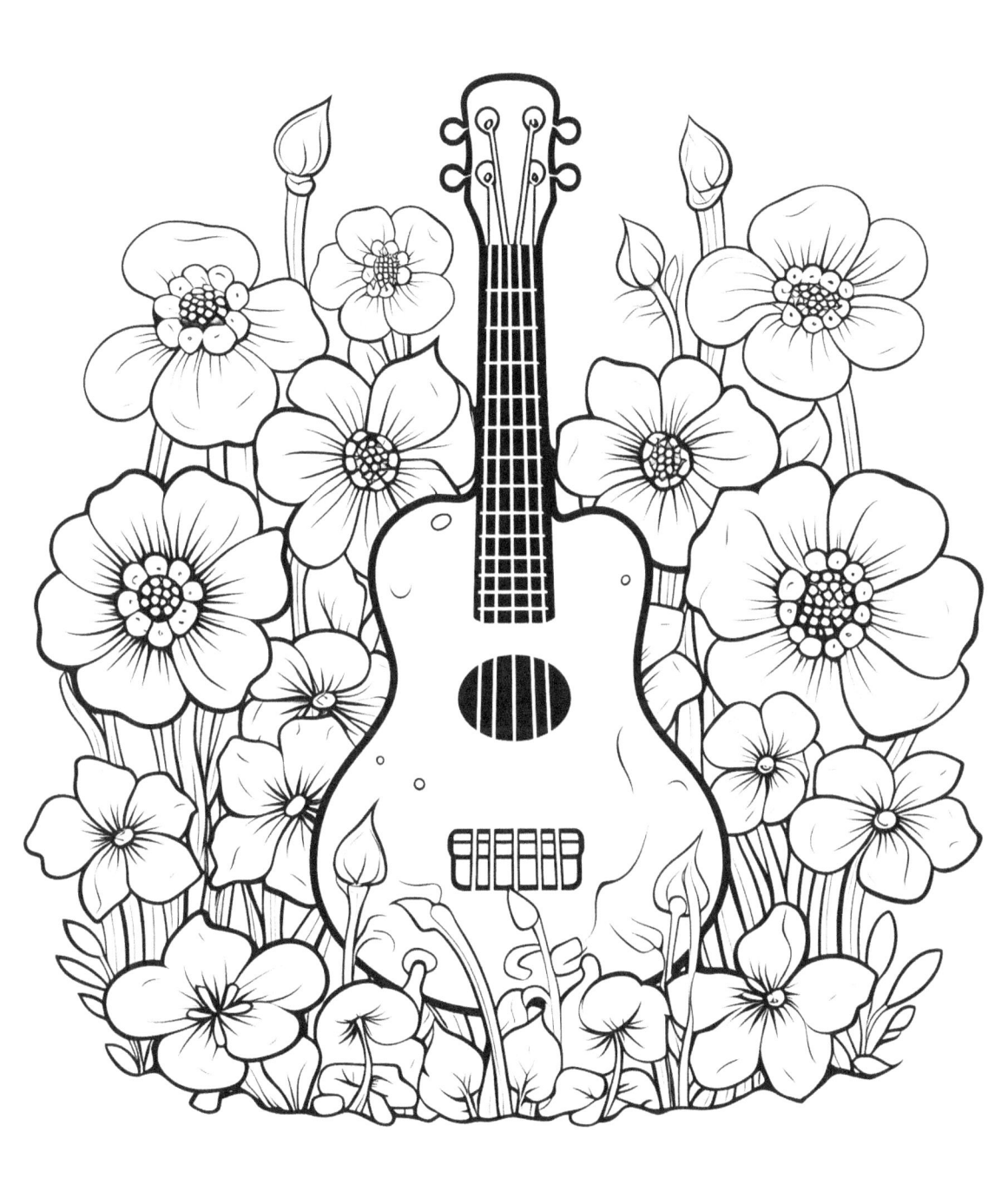

CUP
OF
TEA

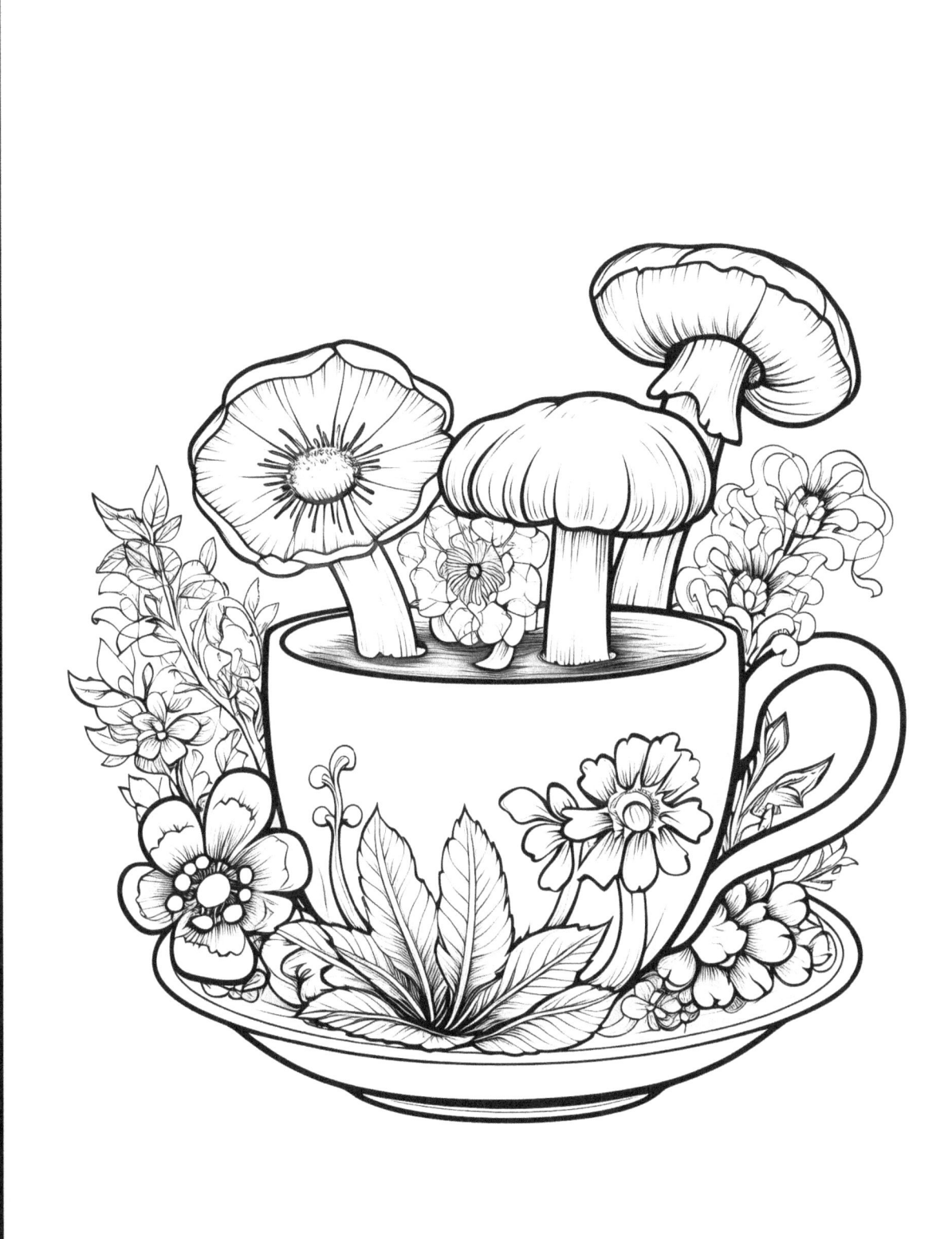

GIRL

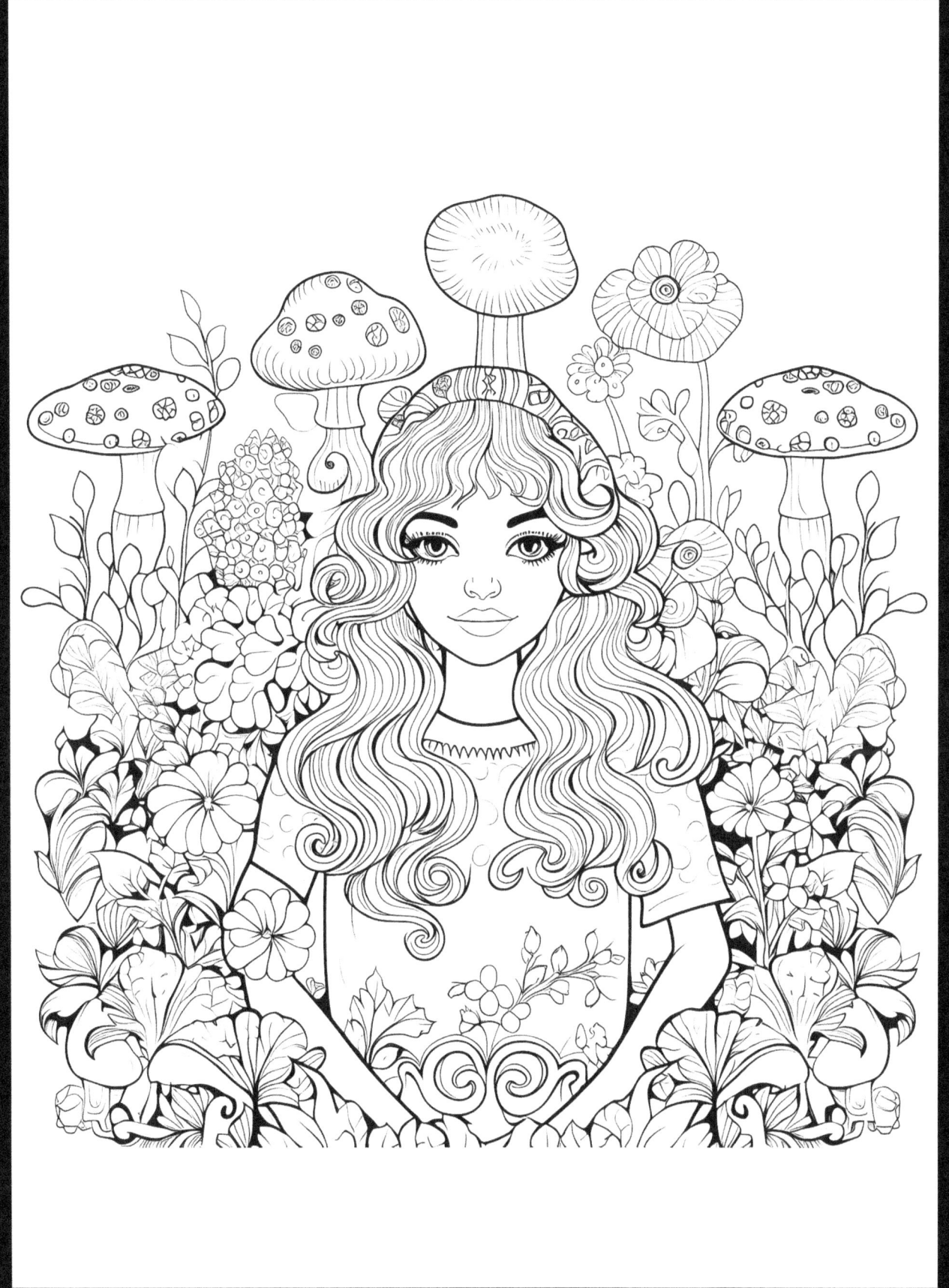

POT
OF
TEA

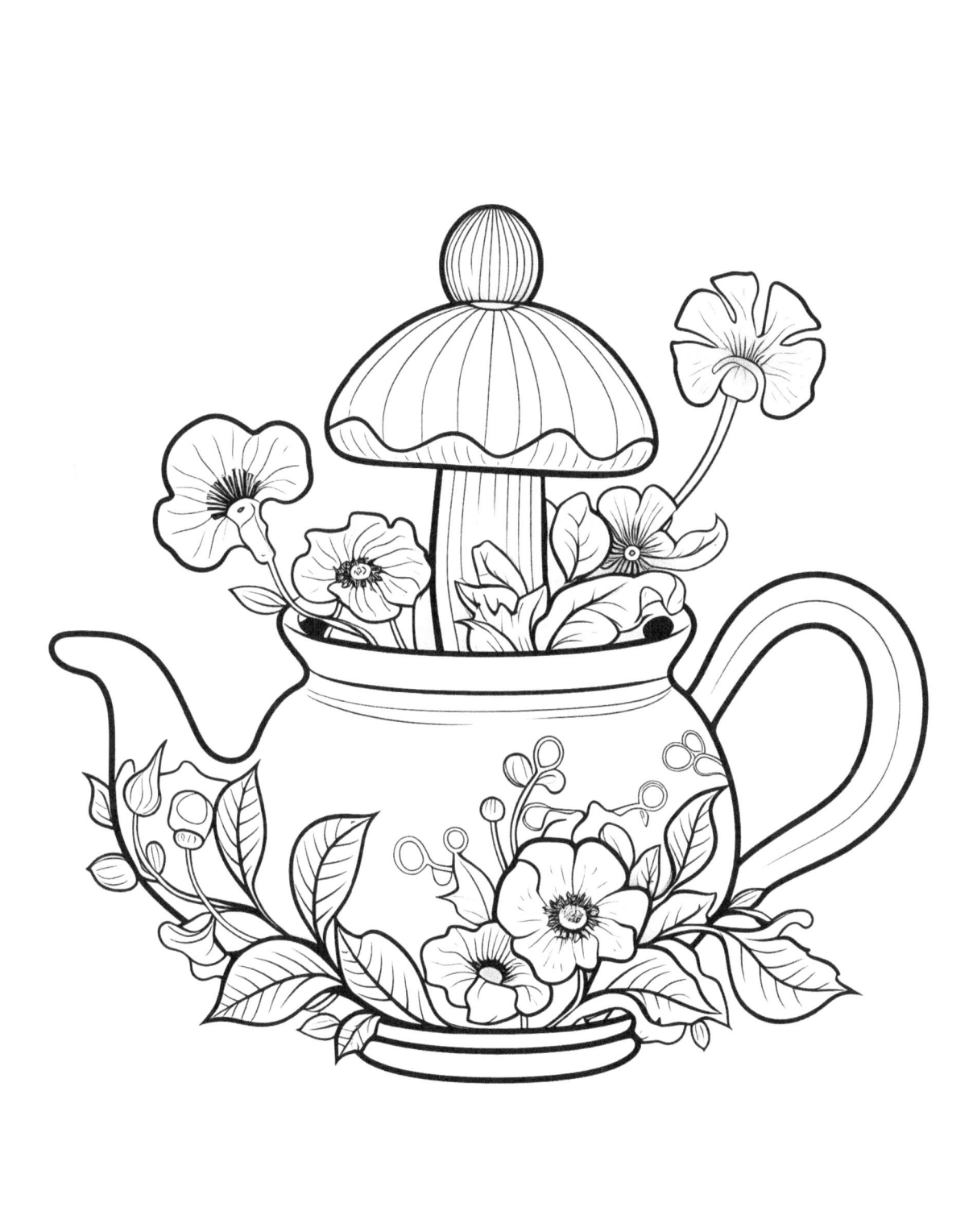

CAMERA

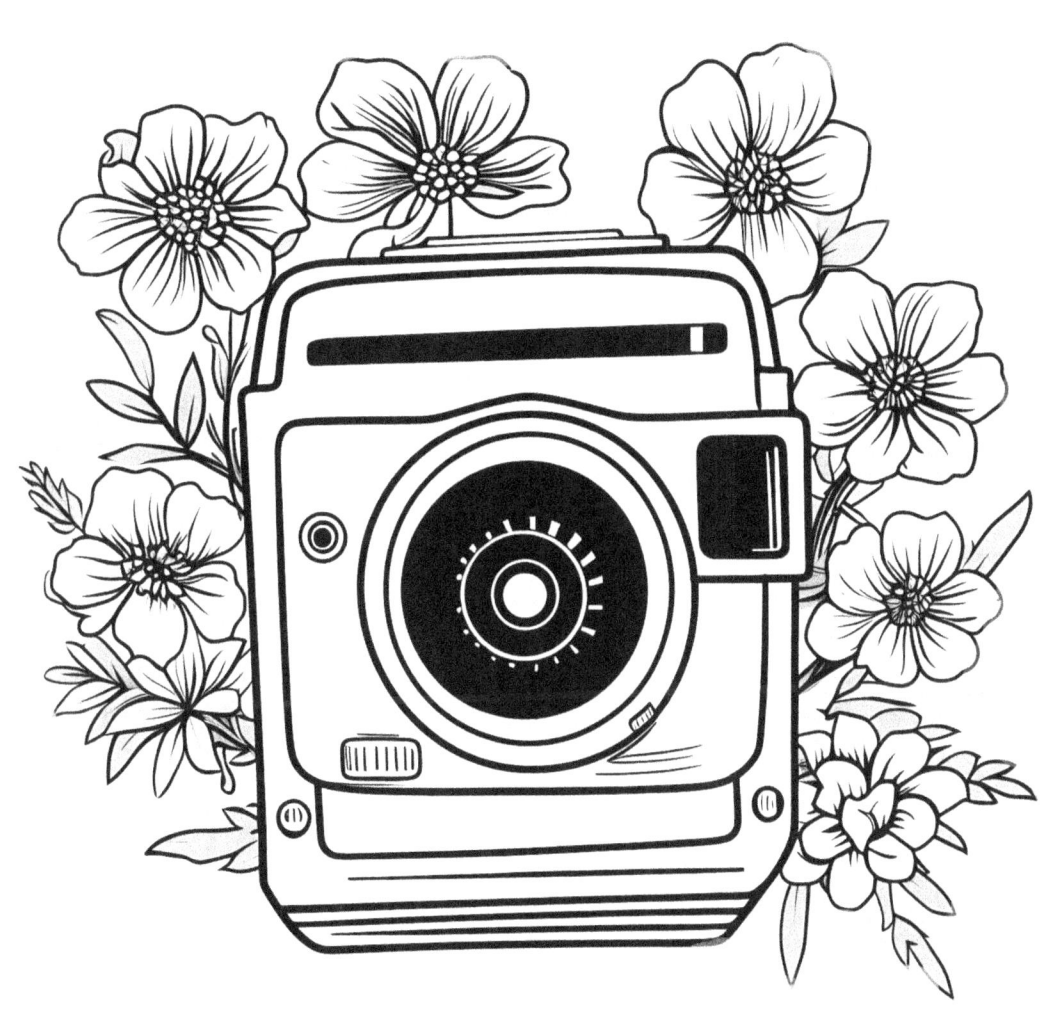

CHANDELIER

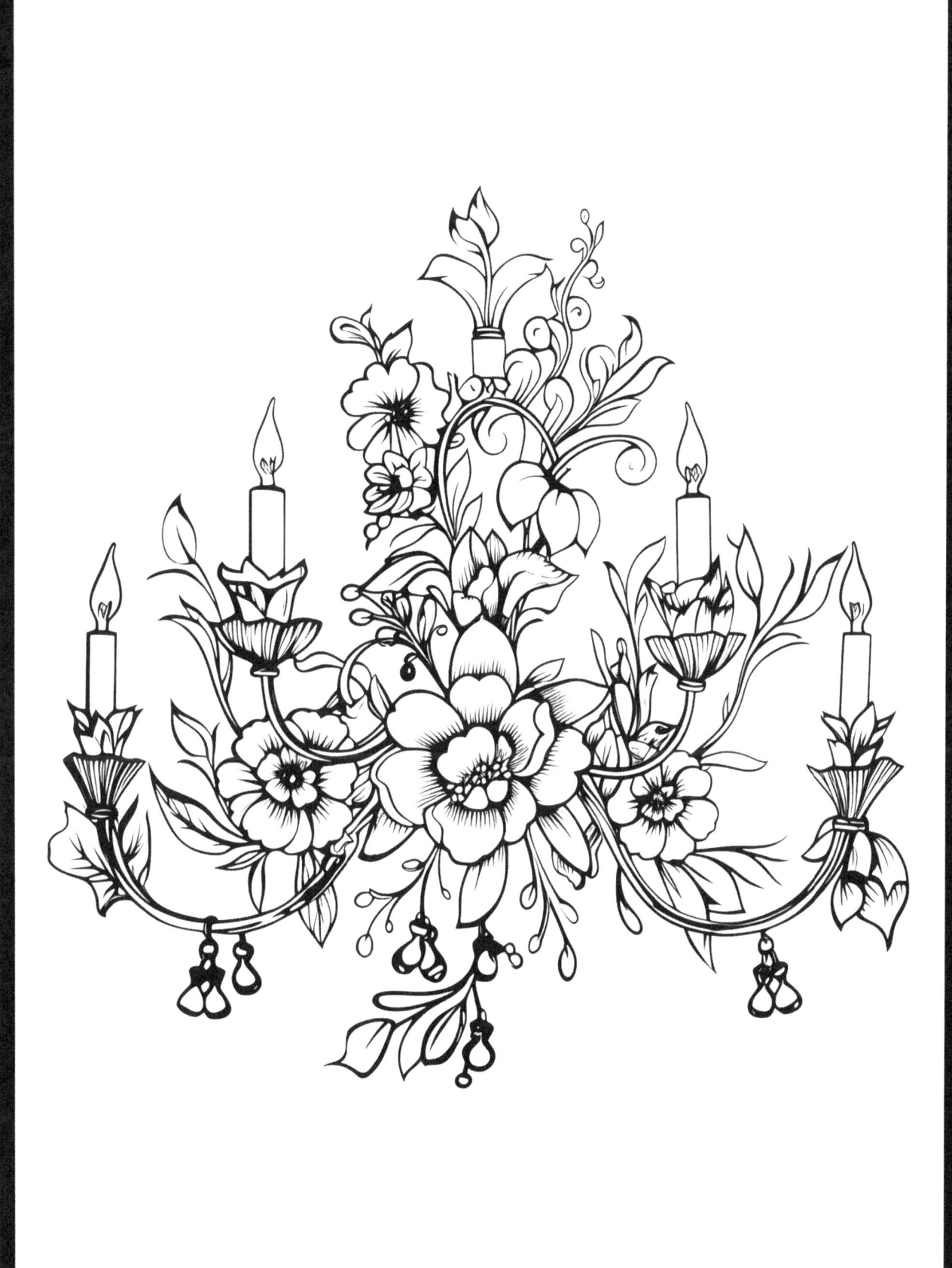

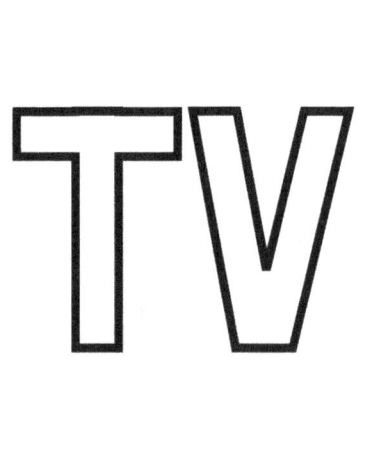

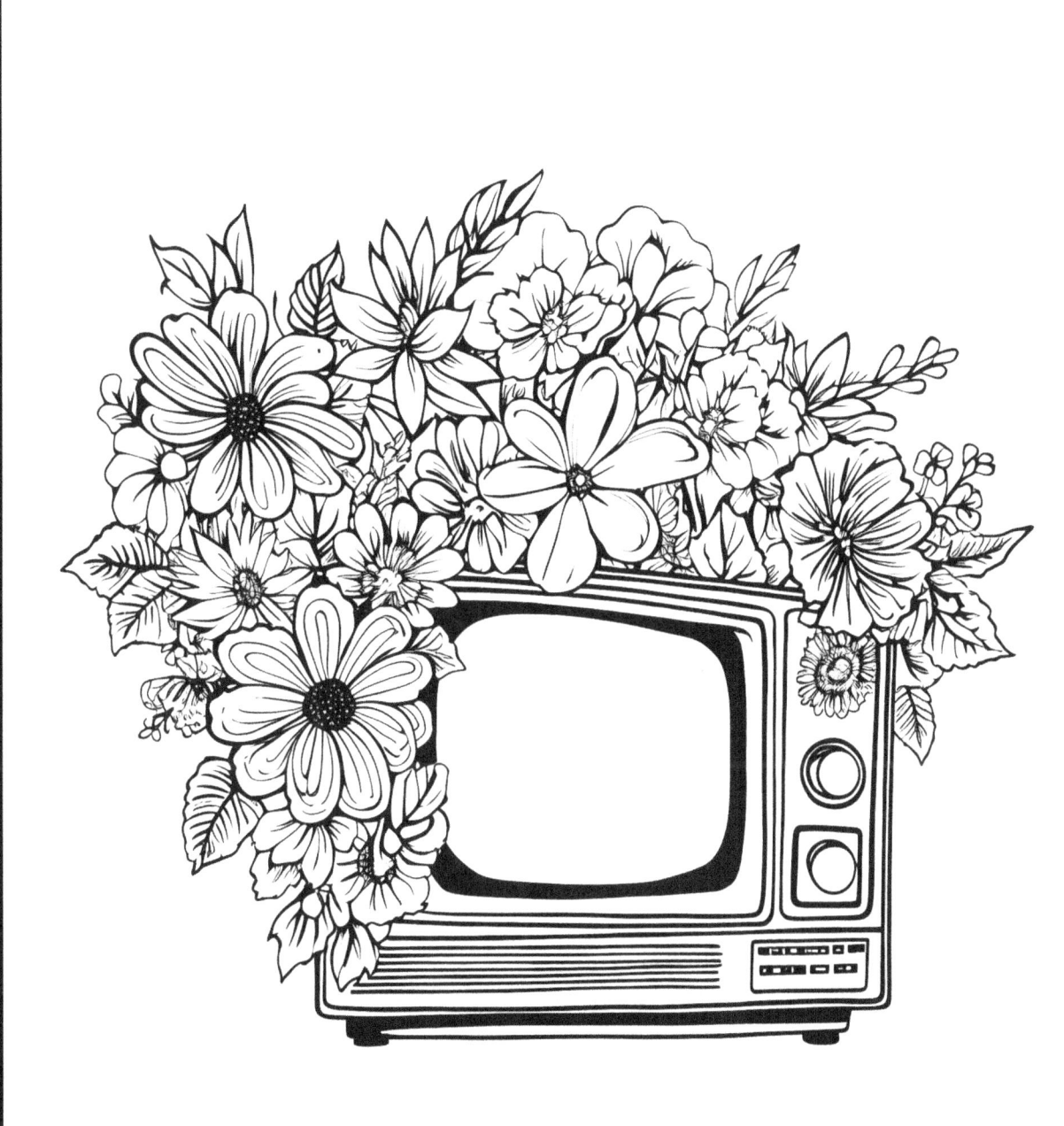

BOOK

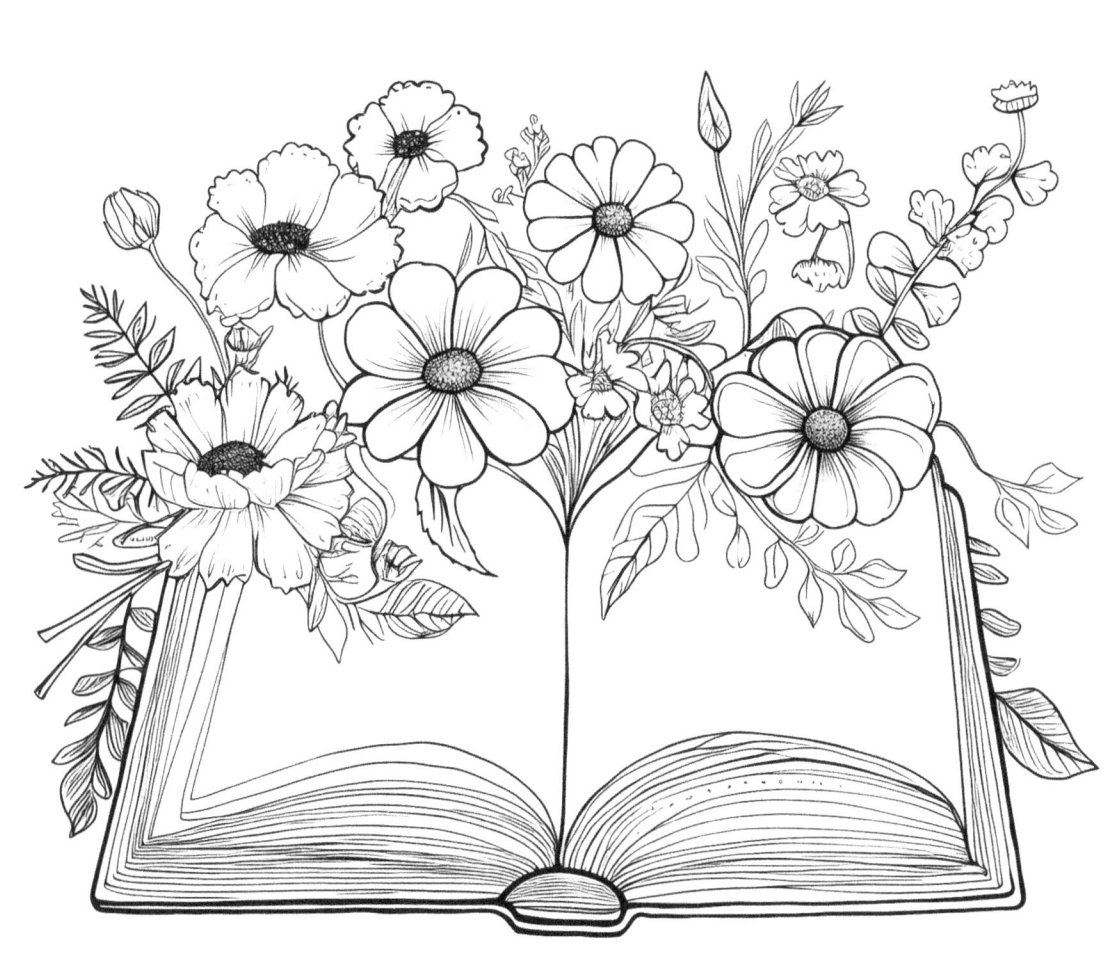

CAMERA

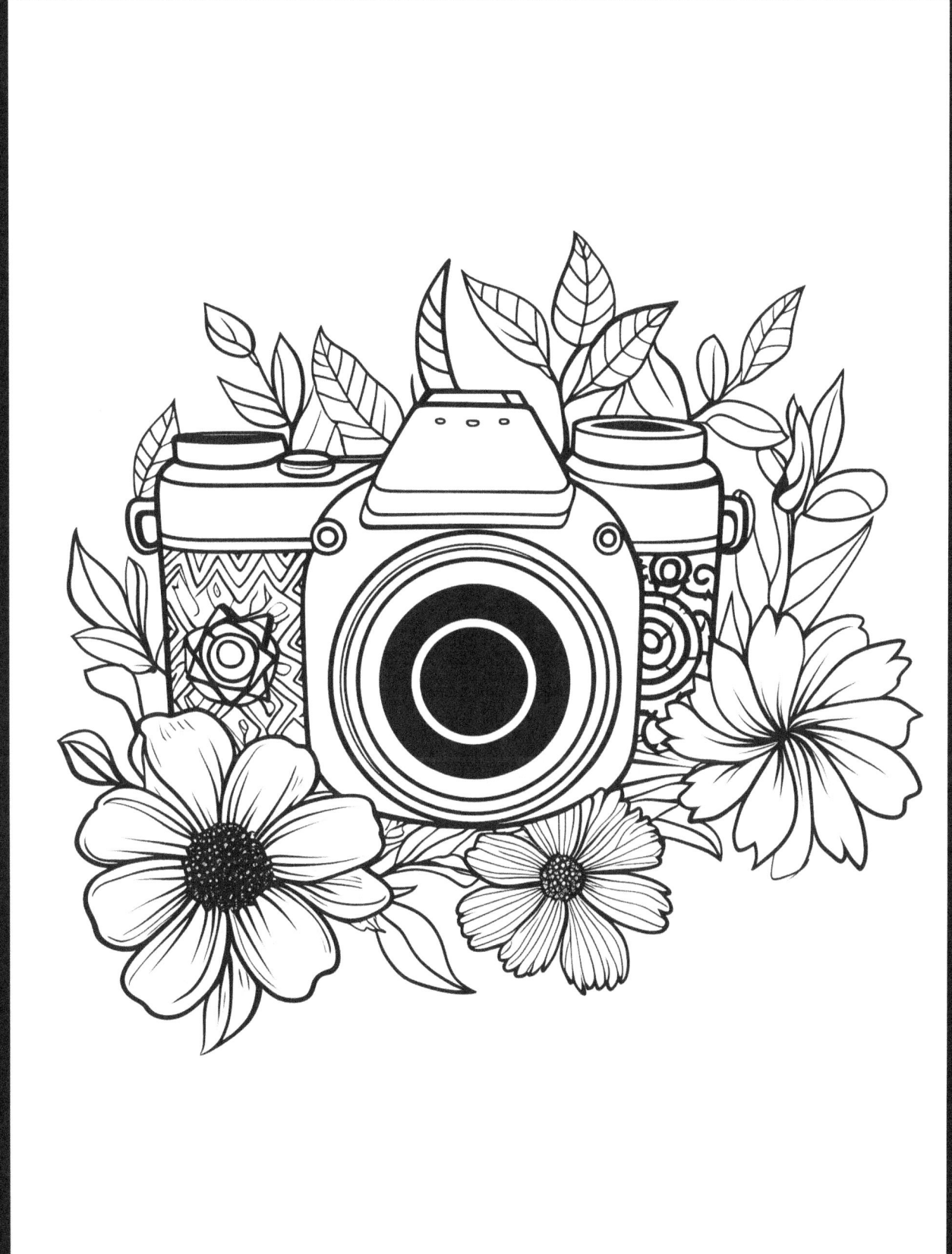

FLOWERS

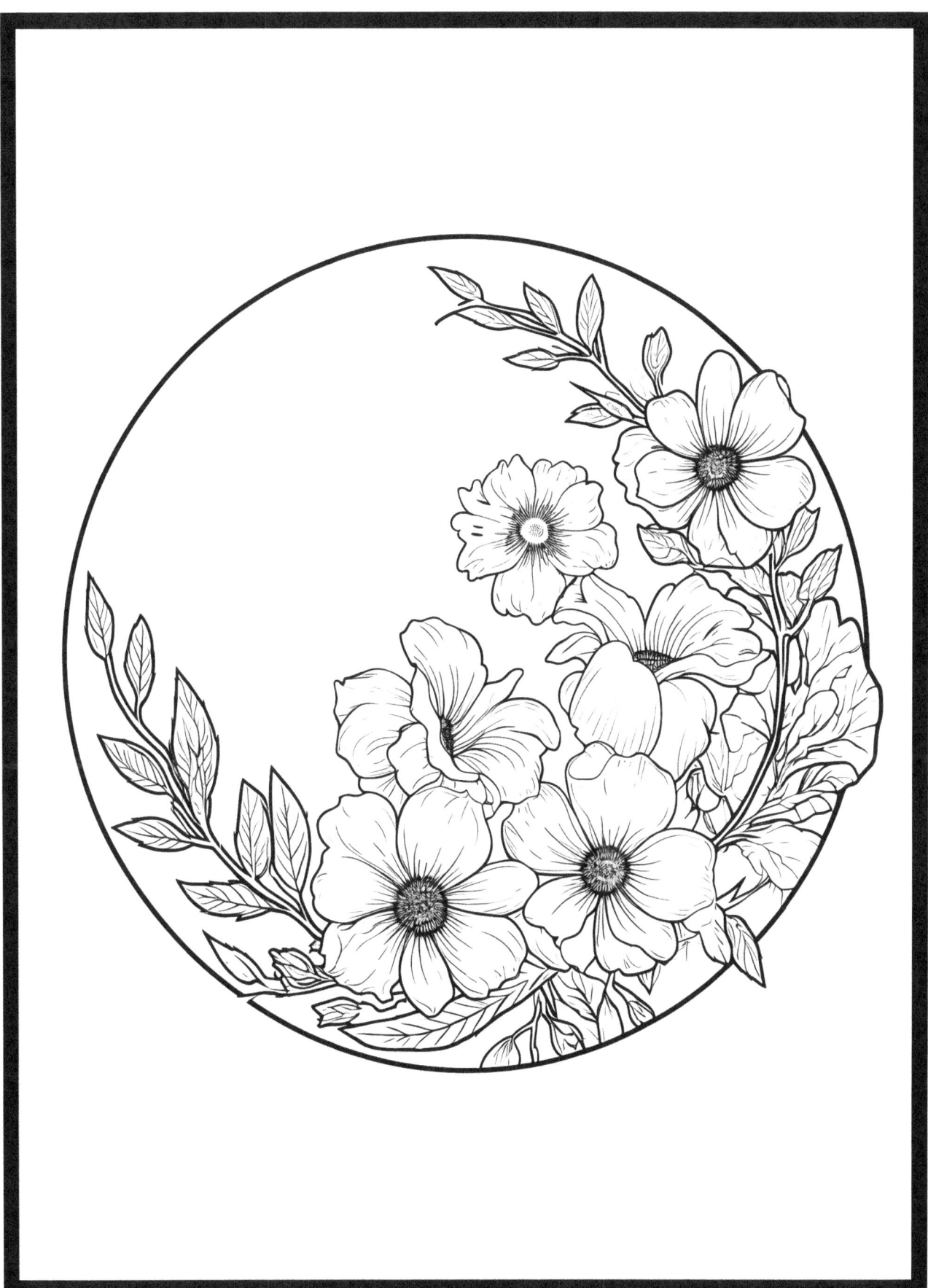

CHAIR

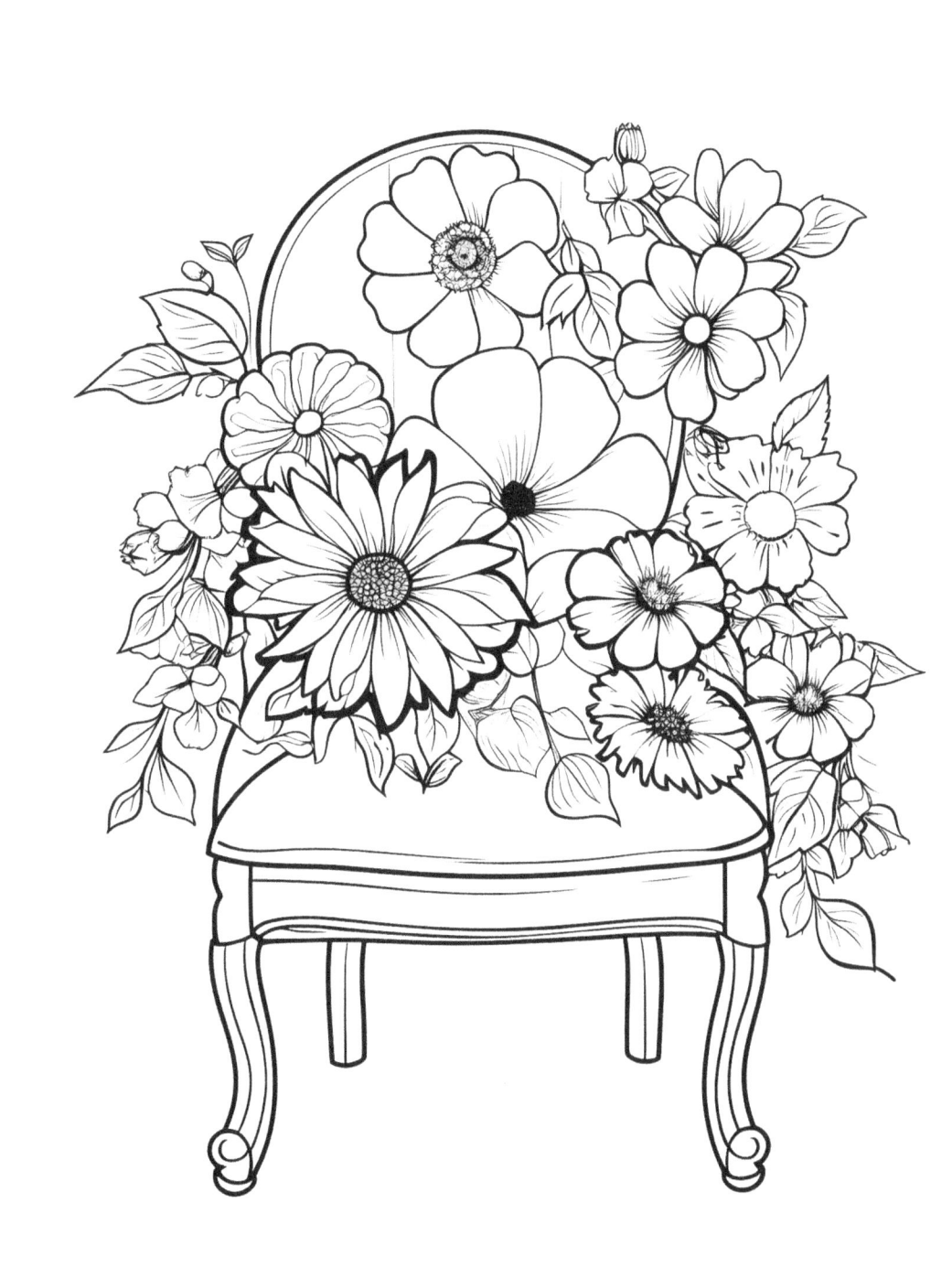

COMPUTER

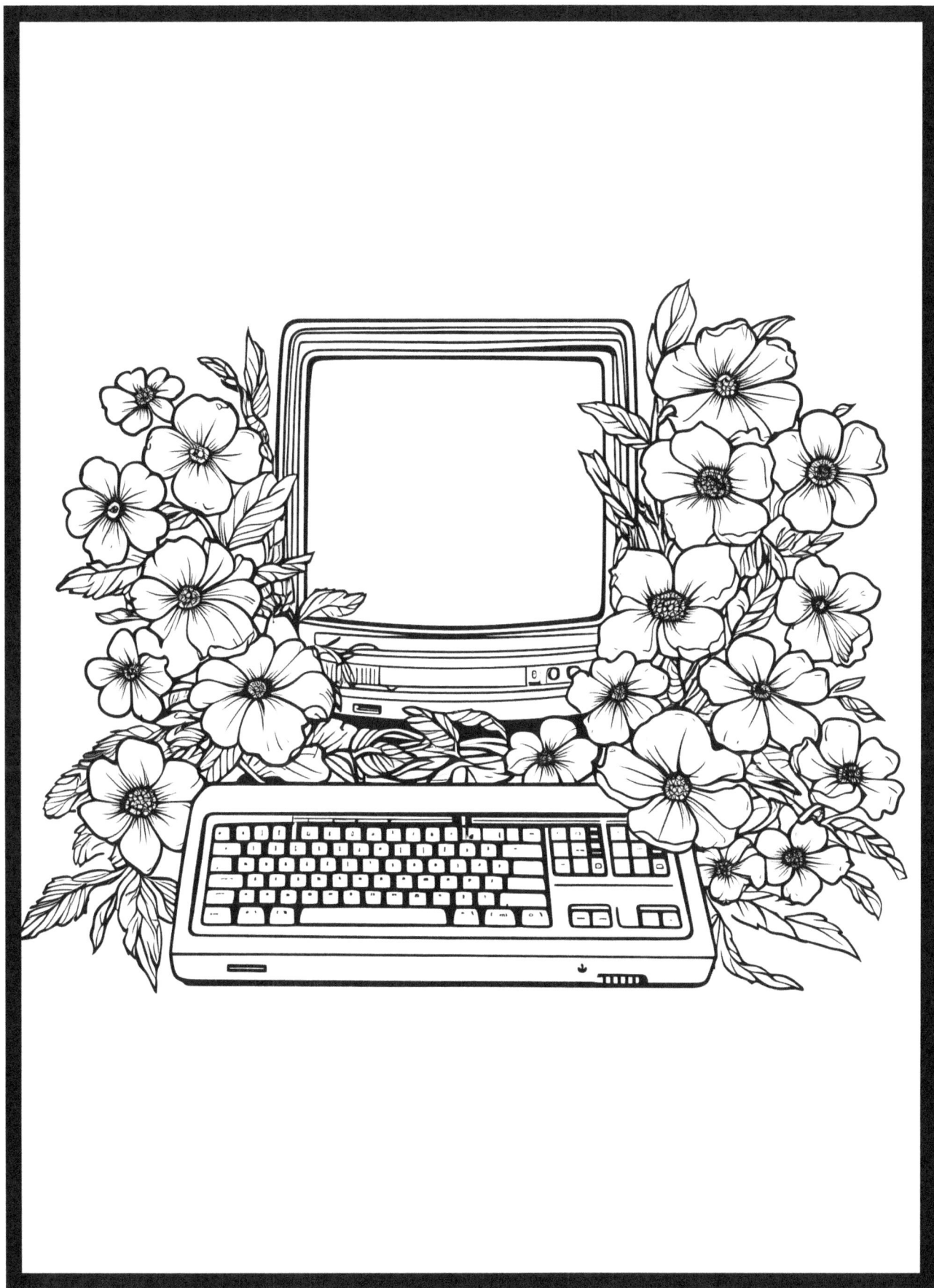

FLOWERS

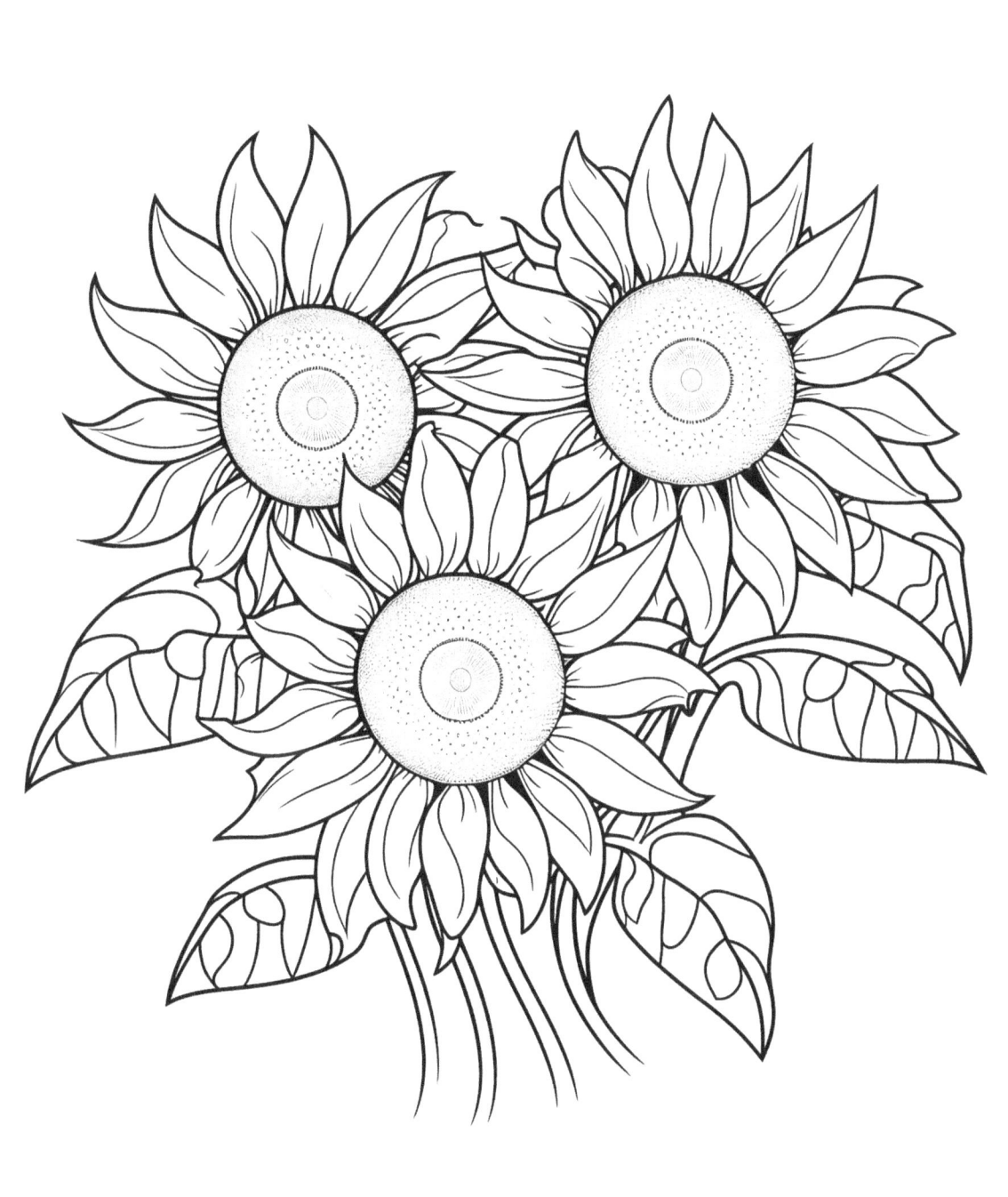

CAT

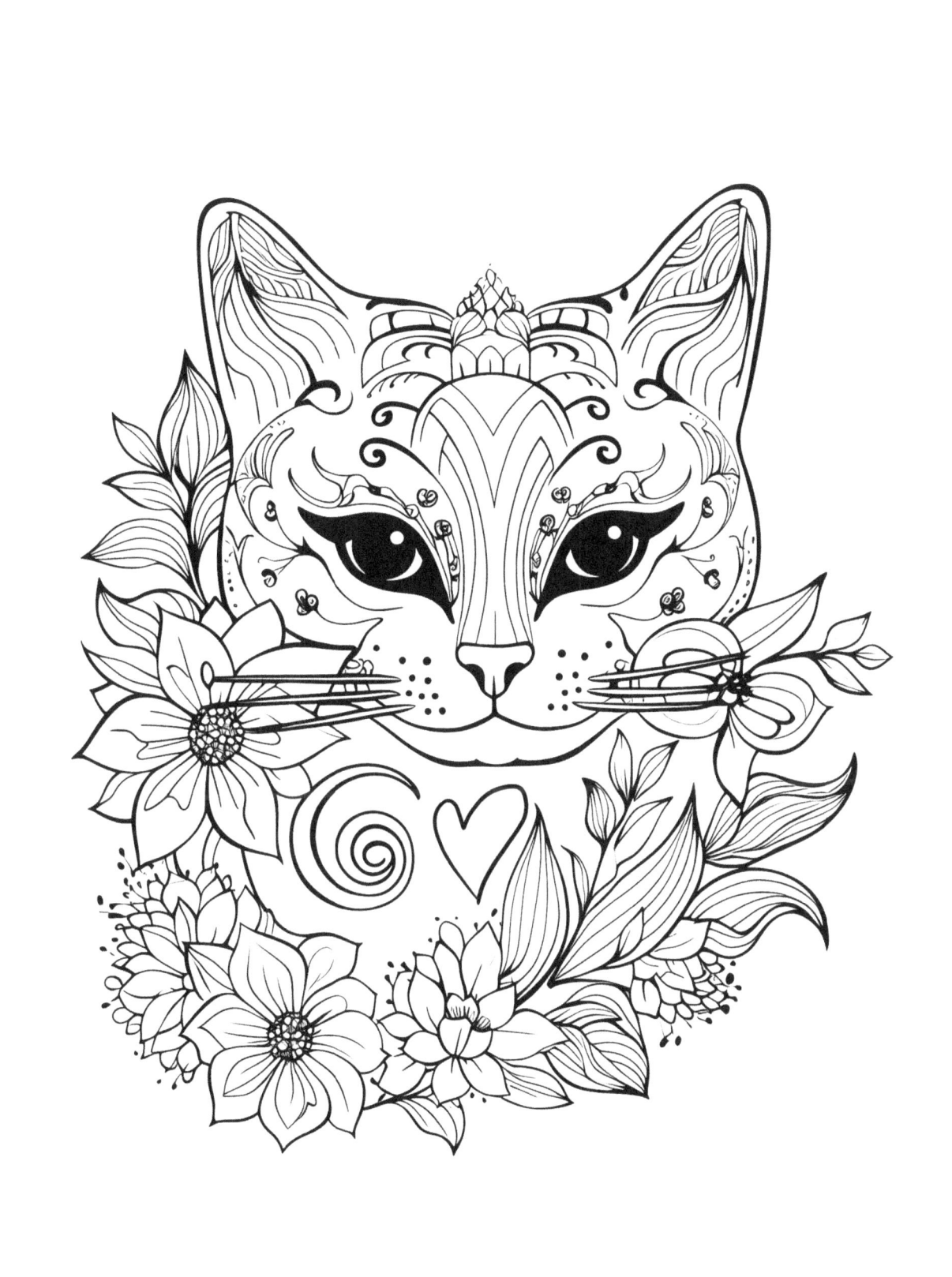

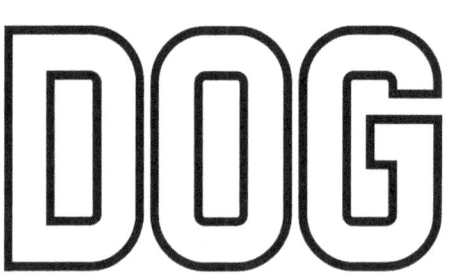

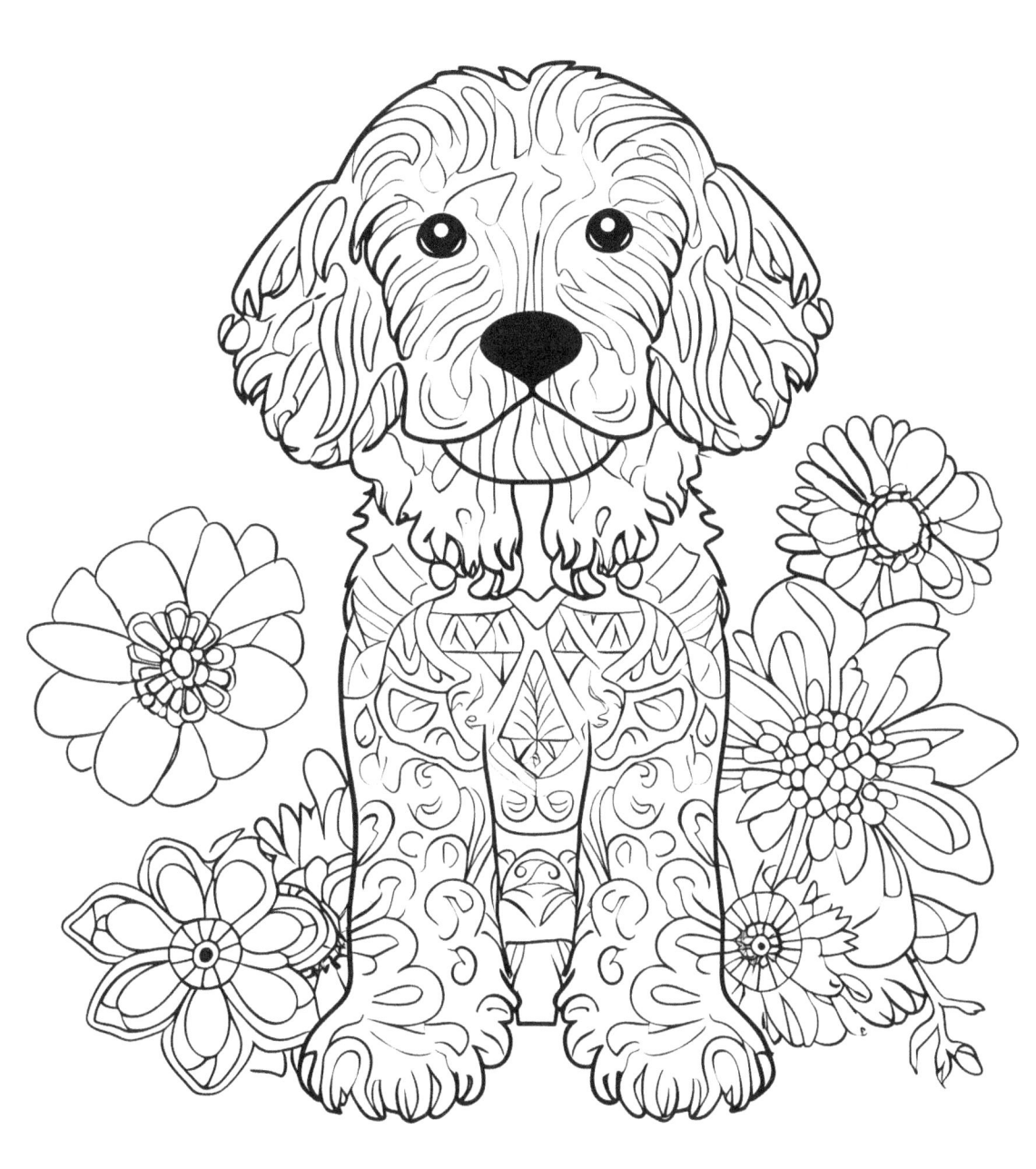

FLOWERS

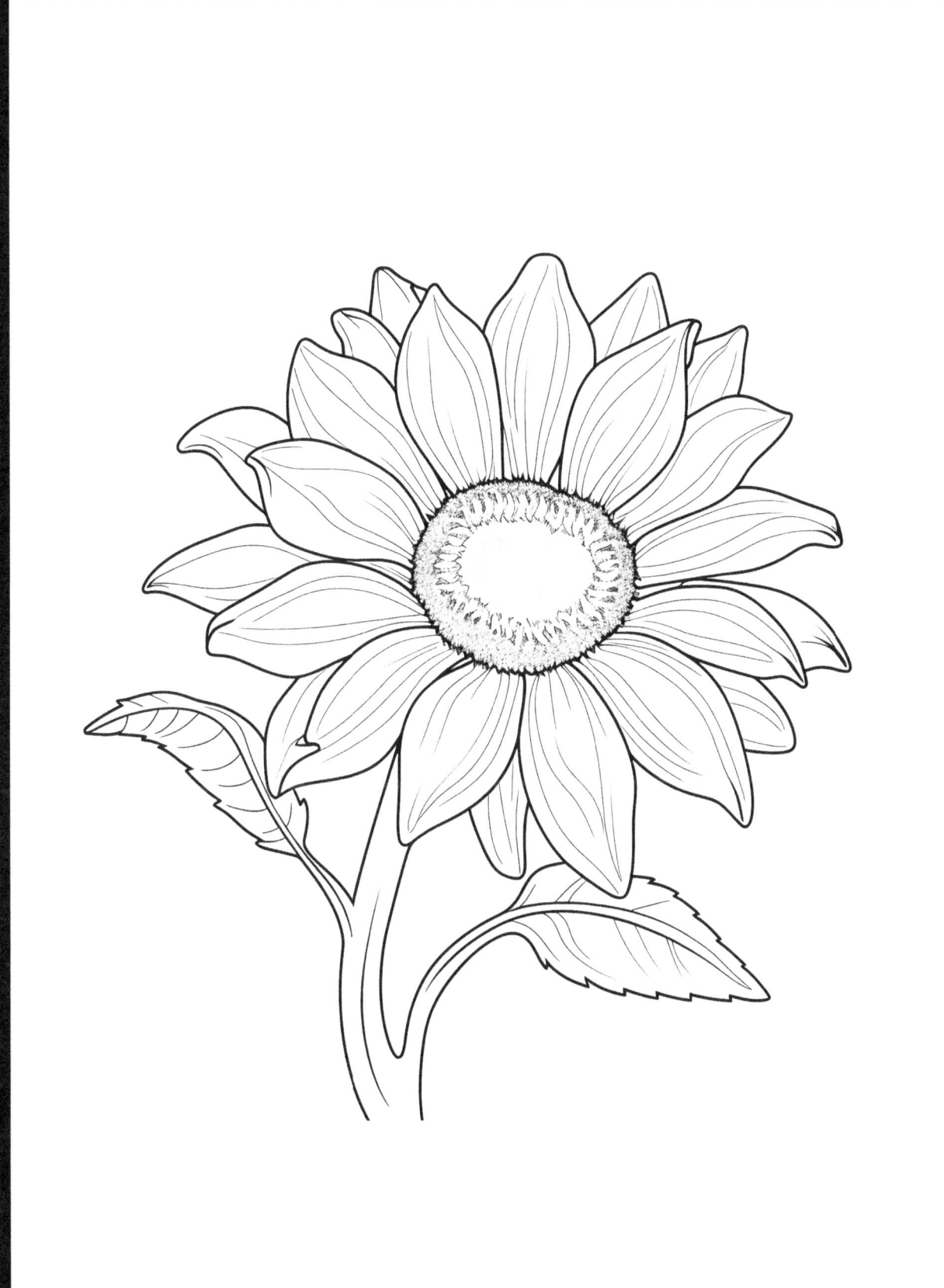

CAT

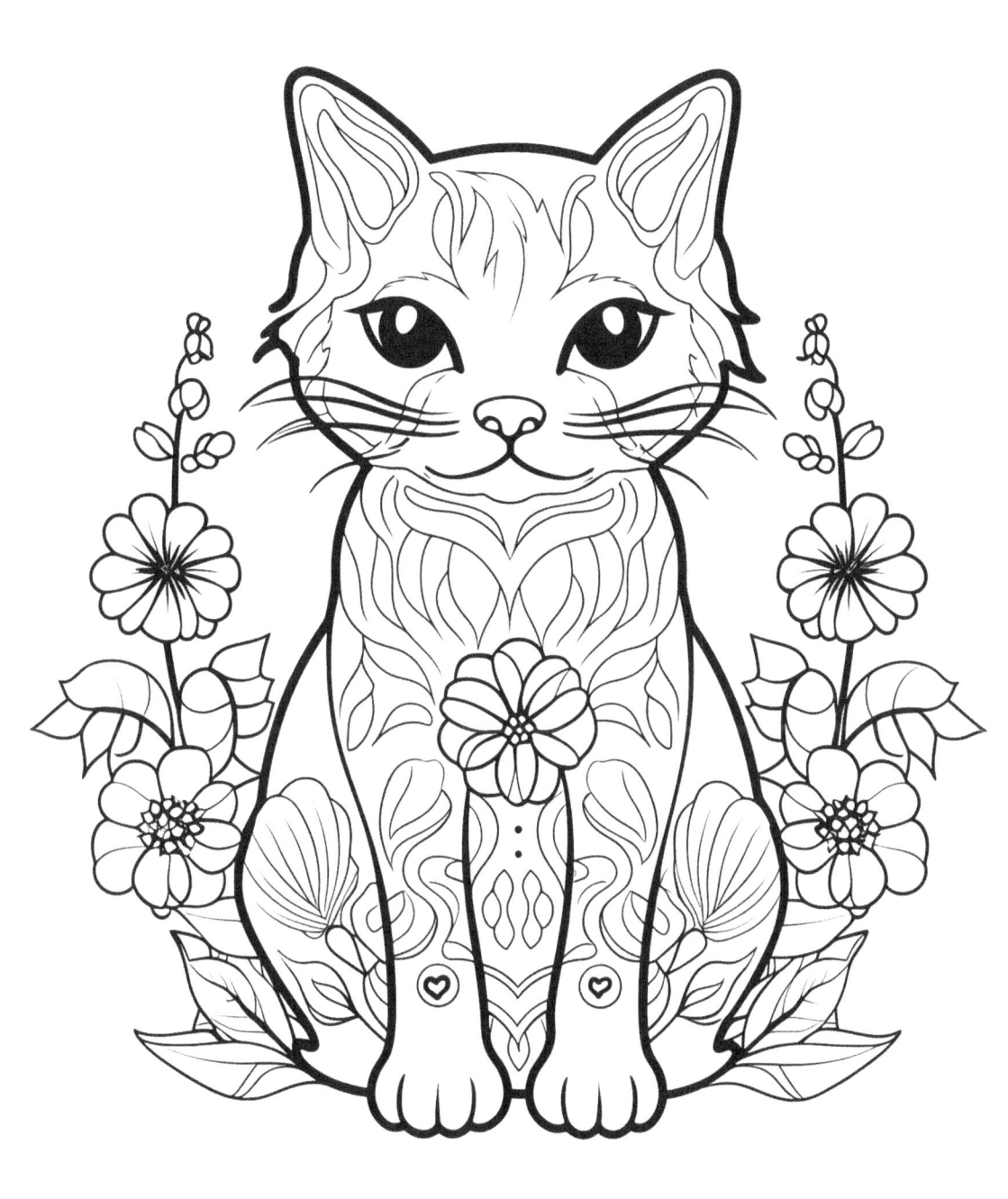

FLOWERS

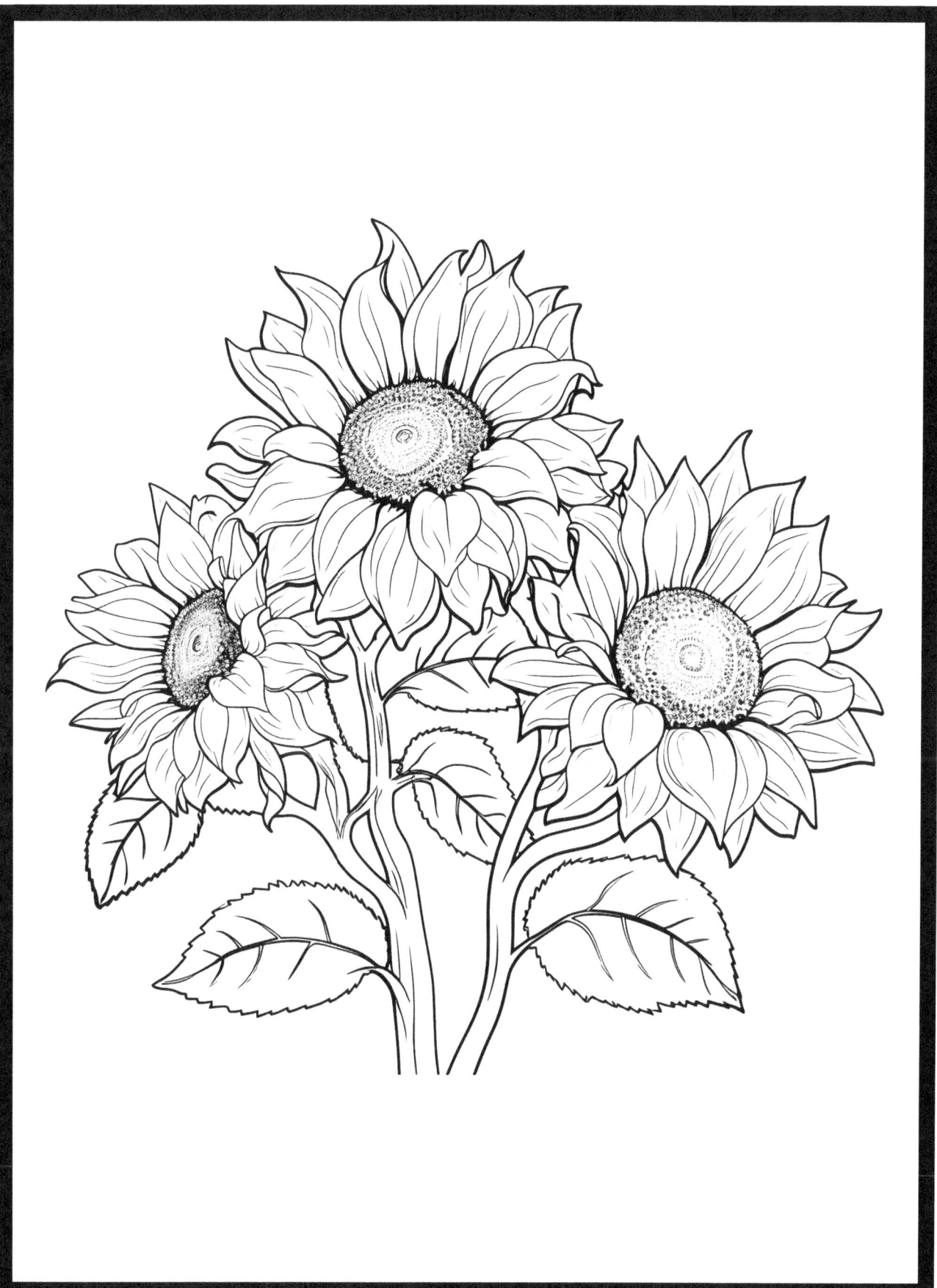

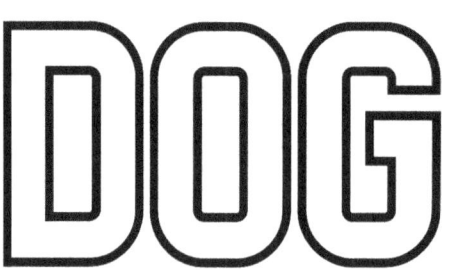

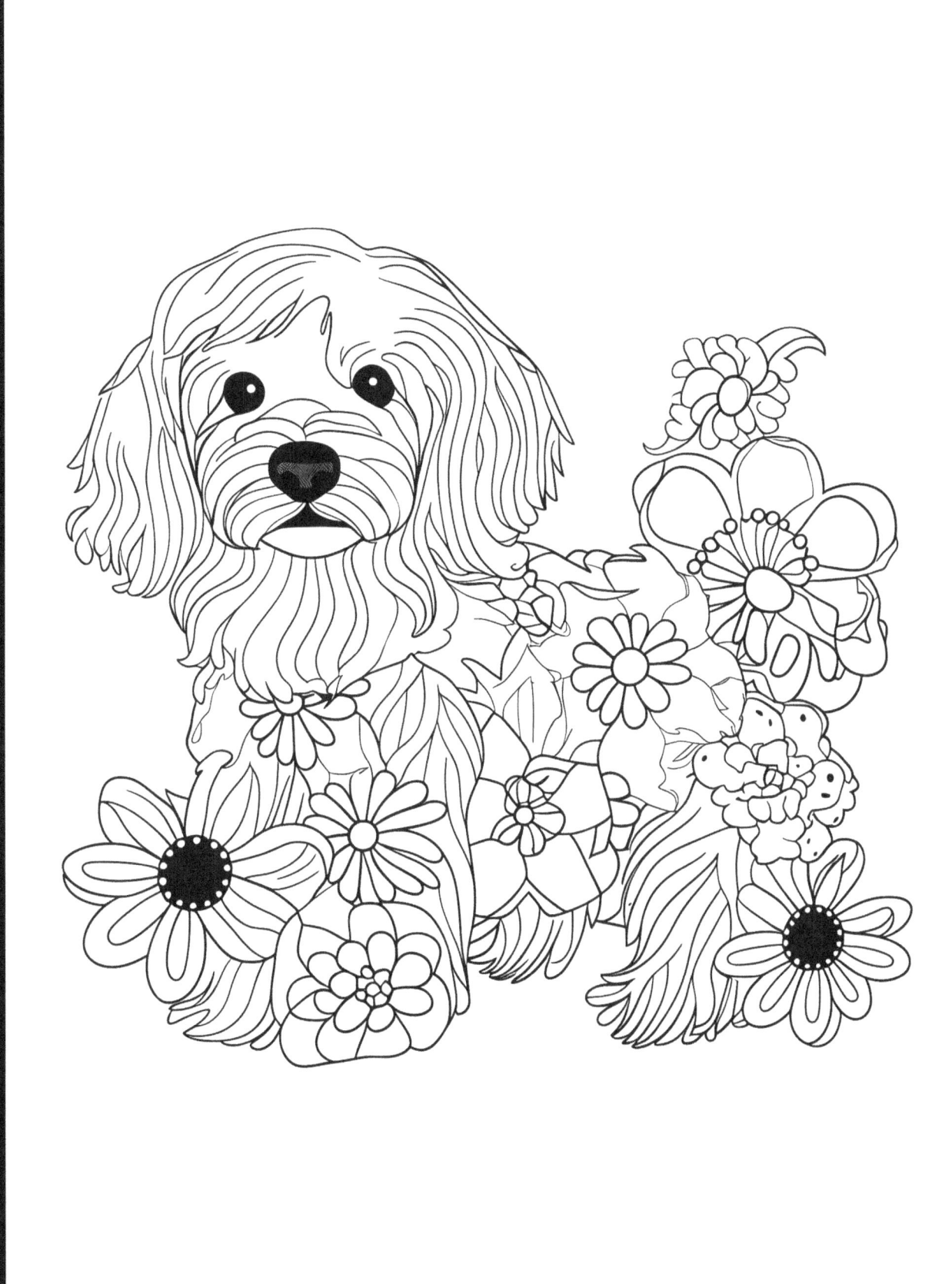

GIRL

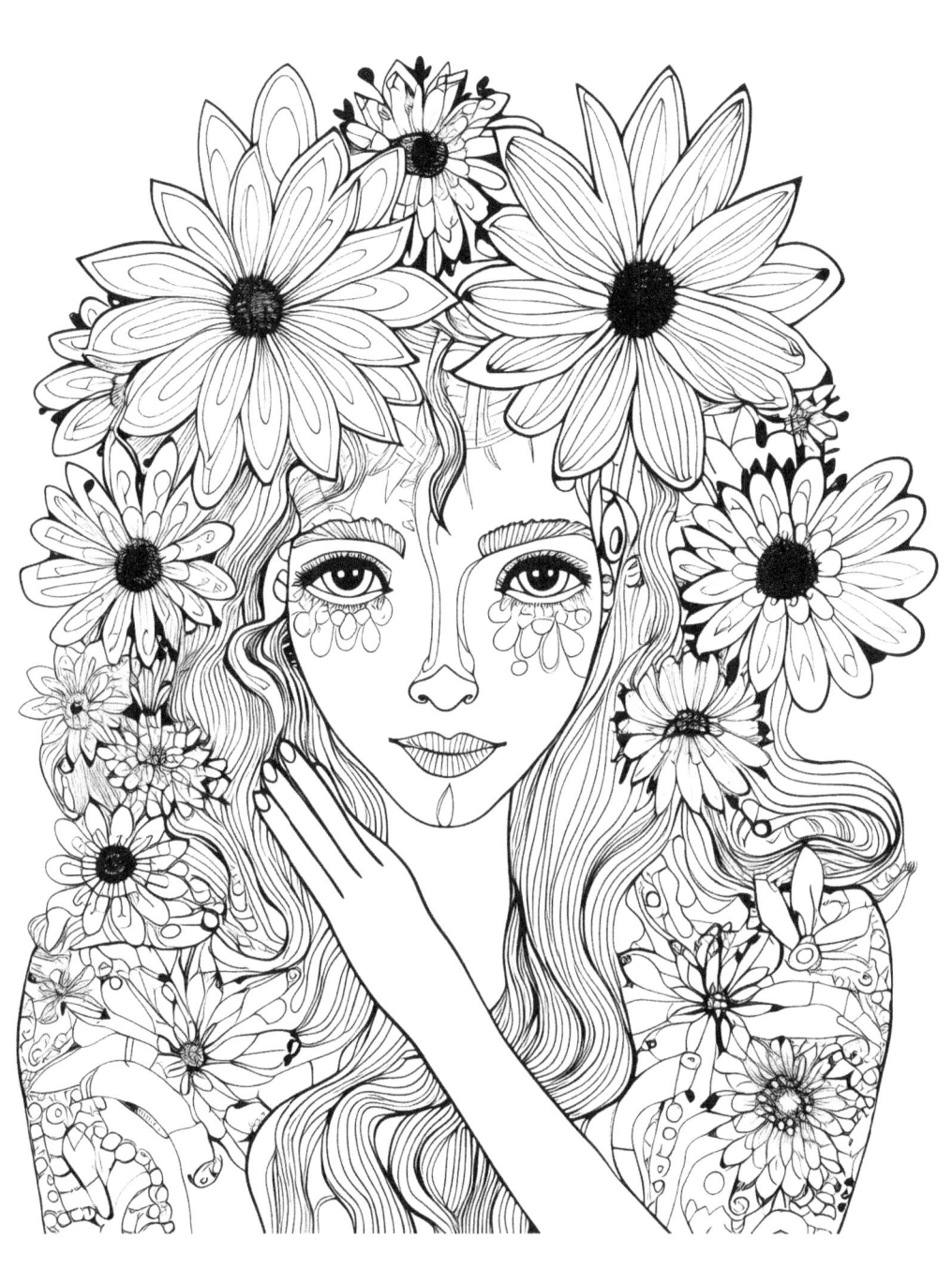

FLOWERS

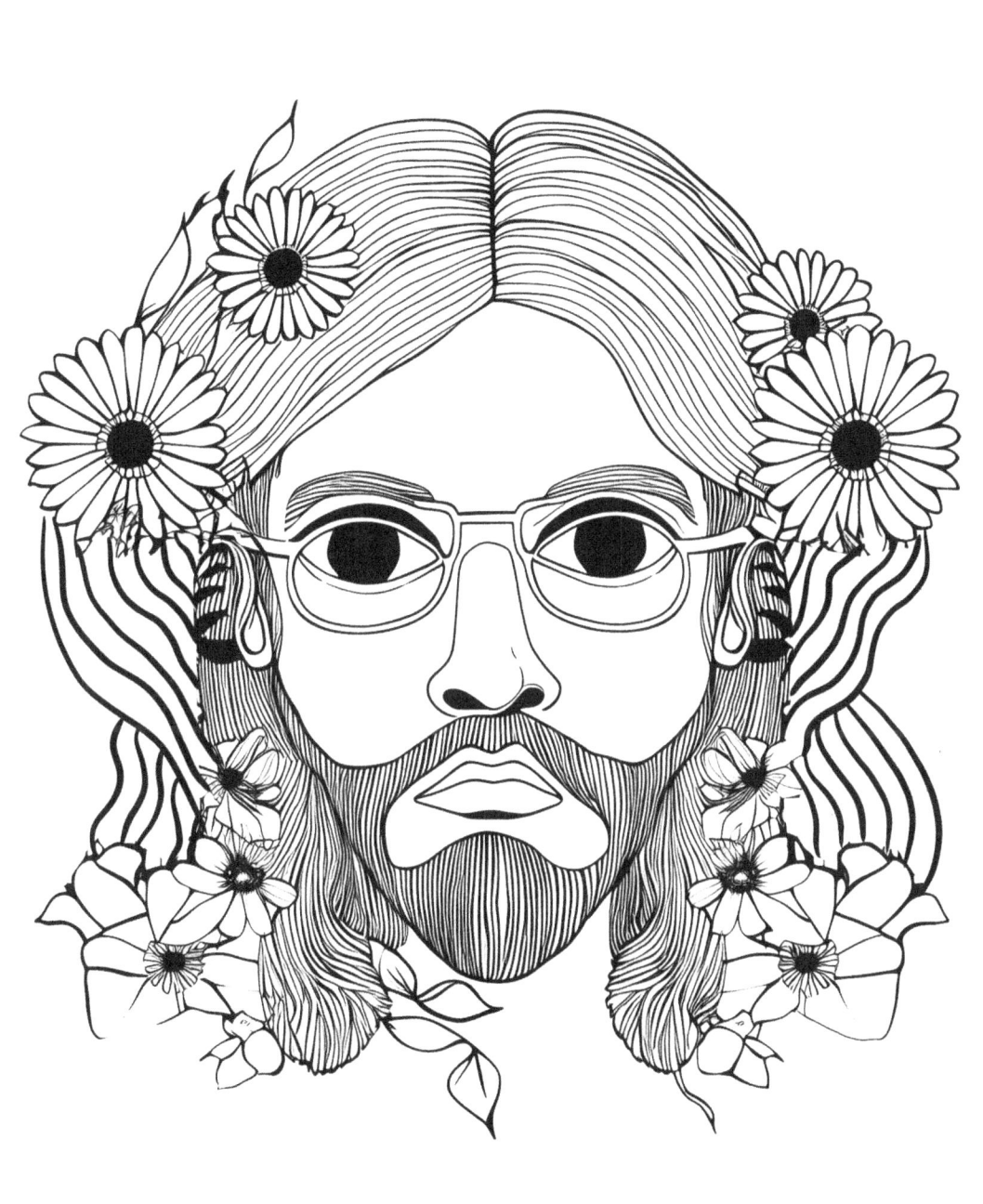

BOOTS

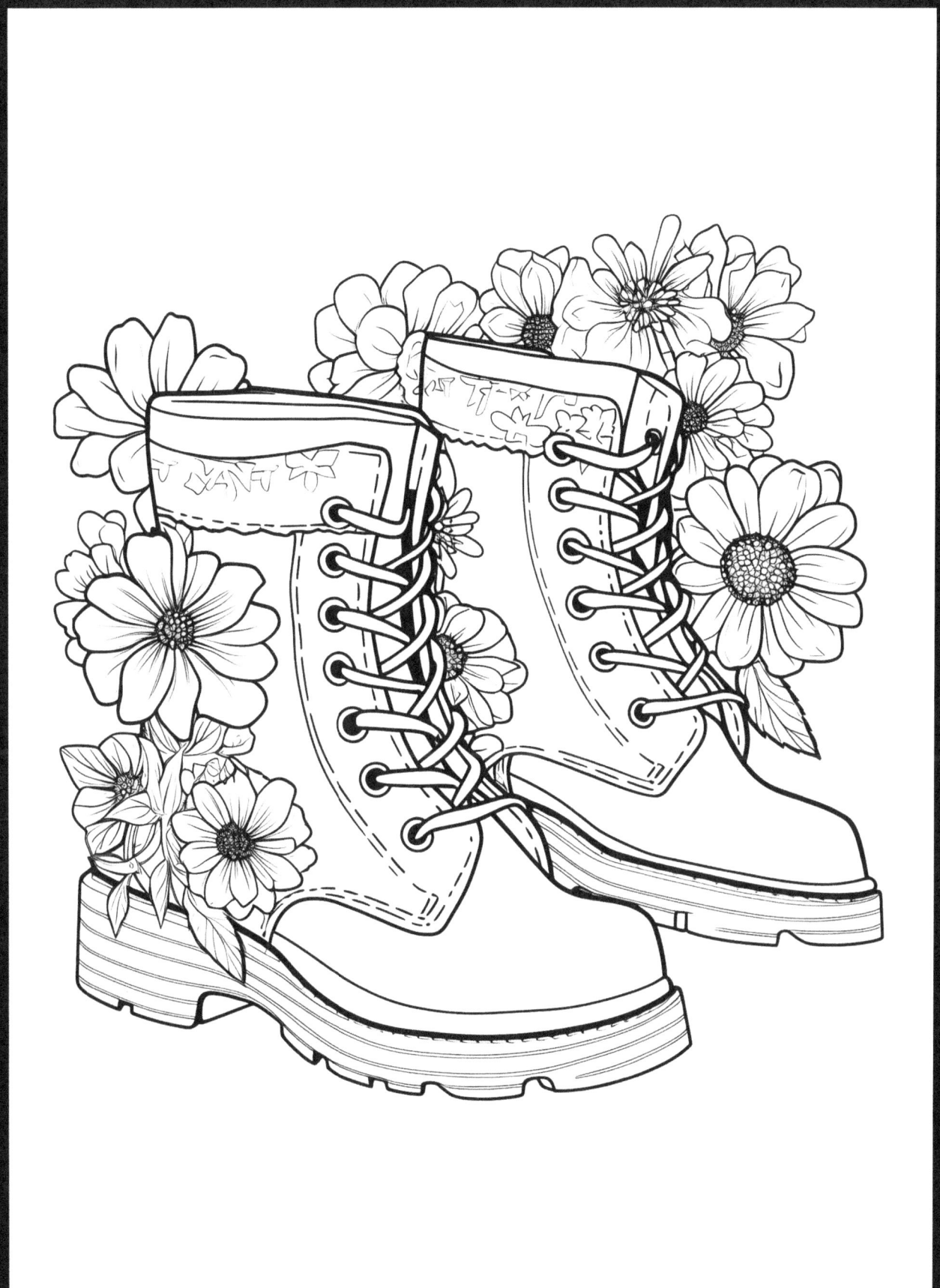

JAR

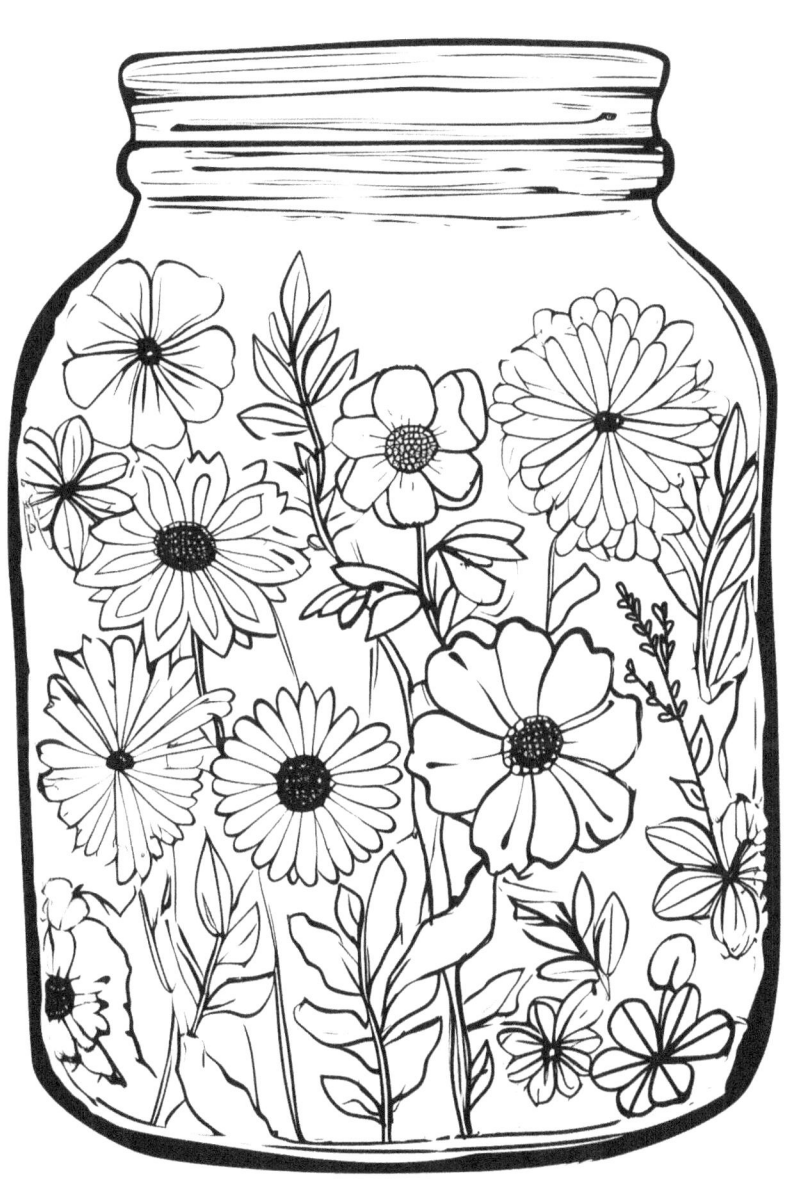

ROSES

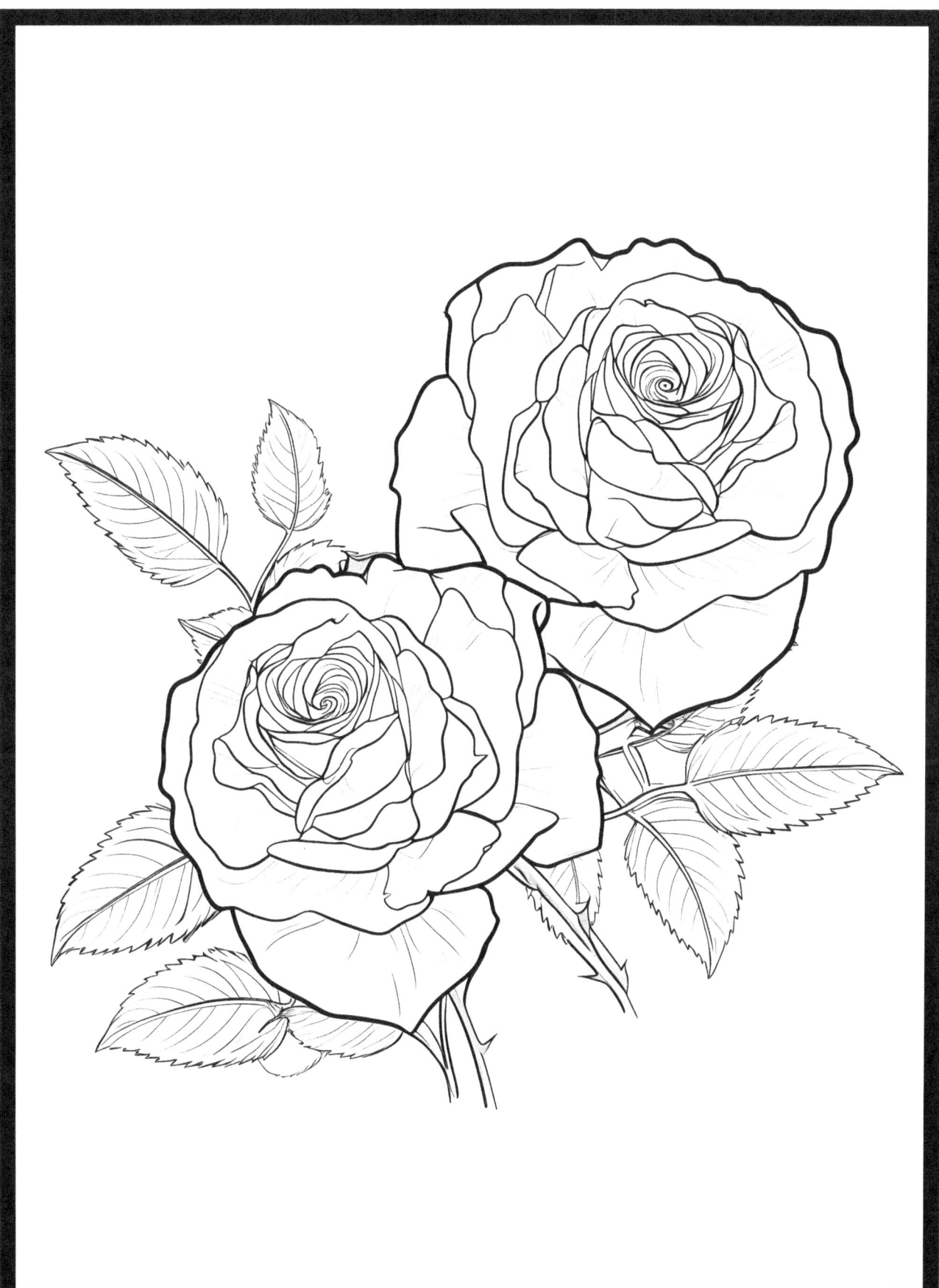

FLOWERS
IN
LIFE